101 Stories of
American History

by Comedian Mike Donovan

Based on True Events

2015 Lashua Press, N.Y.

Fable Of Contents

Fair Warning

Please pardon the intrusion. I know you're eager to dig into the body of this work, but this is not your run-of-the-mill history book and you should know a little bit about the author, Mike Donovan.

Yes, he's a historian, but he is also a comedian.

I could fill pages citing his various comedy credits. Suffice it to say, for the sake of brevity, he has performed stand-up at major venues all over the country and has numerous television credits. He was even considered for a starring role in a television sitcom, but he declined because he didn't respect the premise of the show.

I have had the privilege of sharing the stage with him countless times and I'm proud to consider him a friend. I first met *comedian* Mike Donovan, and then I met *historian* Mike Donovan

I'll never forget visiting his home for the first time back in the early 1990's. I was awestruck. Books lined every single wall from floor to ceiling. I perused the shelves, and nearly every book was related to history. I soon found that I could pull any book from anywhere in the room to find copious notes that Mike had scribbled into the margins.

He went about making coffee for us and, as he reached for a coffee can, I spied even more history books stuffed in the kitchen cabinets. We've spent many late nights discussing history, and his knowledge of the subject appears to be endless.

The vast majority of the stories you are about to enjoy are little known, and all are entertaining. Mike brings historical figures, both large and small, to life within these pages. Just wait until you meet the industrious contortionist Box Brown, the 'scandalous' Peggy Eaton, and – in one of my favorites – the repugnant Surkhano.

Do you know the only two people that FDR ever screamed at?

Do you know why JFK was so afraid of hitting a hole-in-one?

You will soon.

- Steve Bjork; Editor

Author's Introduction

These are the 101 stories of American History that I would most want to tell you if we were just hanging out somewhere. I've been working on a gigantic general History of the United States for the past 11 years, and a few people have wondered who will ever read it because it is so big. So, here is a short book, just to show that I can keep it short.

All the stories are true, but I choose the pen-name 'Comedian Mike Donovan' to let you know that I might joke around with a fact now and then and invent some dialogue. But the jokes do not change the essence of the story one bit. In fact, they accentuate it. Or at least that is my intention. I might even change the name of a very secondary character, as a shout-out to a friend.

This collection is a song of American History. I didn't invent the notes, but I have woven them into a tune. I hope you'll sing along. Some of these stories are funny in and of themselves, some I try to make funny, and some are too serious and beautiful for jokes. I hope you like the mix.

I appear regularly on WBZ radio in Boston as "Historian Mike Donovan" along with host Dean Johnson.

The word 'history' is a simple derivative of 'story.' With this little book (and hopefully some additional volumes in the future, 101 Stories of American History, Volume 22 by 2020) I try to put the story back in history.

One disclaimer: These are all pure American History except one. The story of the French submarine *Surcouf*, lost in WWII, is an exception I let sneak in because it fascinates me. But *Surcouf* is really more a part of French history than American. Le supersub is part of American history only in that an American merchant ship accidentally destroyed it, and because the loss of the *Surcouf* changed the way De Gaulle's Free France related to America for the rest of the war and beyond.

This is my first book, first edition.

Steve Bjork, my editor, saved me from myself. If he hadn't spotted my mistakes this book would be hilarious for all the wrongs reasons.

Mike Donovan
Pt. Barrow Alaska
September 2015

1
The Heckler on the Mayflower

There were 20 professional sailors among the 102 passengers on the *Mayflower* in 1620. These pros were neither Pilgrim nor adventurer and their names are lost to history. But one of them in particular took it upon himself to ridicule the Pilgrims constantly; and he added a lot of swearing, which horrified them so much more. If you were a sick Pilgrim lurching over the side rail, you could be sure to find this sadistic clown right there laughing and calling you names. He was young, healthy, experienced, cruel and arrogant. He actually told the Pilgrims that half of them wouldn't survive the trip, and that he couldn't wait for the opportunity to start heaving their dead bodies overboard!

The Pilgrims hated him, even though most of them lied to themselves by claiming to still love him in the name of the Lord. But, come on. 400 years after the fact, I hate this guy just reading about him.

Halfway across the Atlantic, guess who is the one passenger on board to get seriously ill? Yes, it's 'Dice Clay 1620' who develops a sudden, mysterious and terrible illness. The big-mouth bully is the first to die out of them all, and they hurled his body overboard. Most of them managed to suppress their delight. But Myles Standish couldn't resist saying that, "Sinners like him do not groweth on trees. They hangeth from them."

The Pilgrims presumed that the Lord was punishing the sailor, and they may have been right.

2
<u>Billy Blackstone - 1623</u>

At one time, a wealthy hermit named William Blackstone, or Blaxton, was the only European resident of the Shawmut Peninsula, which later became the city of Boston. Billy had a nice hut on prestigious Beacon Hill.

Reverend Blackstone, an Anglican, was living there all alone and happy when in 1623 a delegation of Puritans living in nearby Charlestown came by to visit and asked him if he would mind some company. The water supply at Charlestown was poor and they felt that the peninsula Blackstone inhabited would be safer and healthier.

Blackstone was a good sport about it and allowed the Puritans to come and share the peninsula with him. His hermit days were over, and in 1630 the Shawmut Peninsula became the City of Boston.

The Puritans, however, soon turned on Blackstone. They didn't agree with all of his religious practices so they burned his house down. Ingratitude was their attitude. I wish I was making this up.

Blackstone moved/fled south to what later became Rhode Island. He set the pattern for Roger Williams, who later got chased out of Massachusetts and made Rhode Island an official haven for those wanting to escape either religious persecution or annoying accents.

The Blackstone River is named after him, but sometimes I wonder if Boston itself isn't also named after him. Sounds pretty close to Blaxton, if you ask me. Sure, the official version is that the city is named after the town of Boston, England, but still I wonder. America is named after Amerigo Vespucci.

3
Tom Morton – Eat, Drink, and Be Merrymount - 1642

Besides Mass Bay, Plymouth, and what was left of Wemagusset Colony, there was also the little colony of Merrymount, which was in today's Quincy, Massachusetts. Two adventurers set up shop there with a few servants. One of them decided to move on to Virginia, but the other one stayed.

The one who stayed was a pettifogger named Thomas Morton. At least some people called him that - and you are going to have to look that word up, just like I did.

Morton became a one-man colony, and what a liberal place it was. It was like the parents were away for the weekend. Merrymount was indeed merry. Morty's Merrymount had freedom *from* religion, which is far more progressive than freedom *of* religion. Morton didn't quarrel with the Indians, he partied with them. He drank with them, played games of chance with them, learned their language, and slept in their long houses.

In short, he was cool.

Instead of building defensive walls at English Merrymount, Morton built an 83-foot tall maypole and invited the Indians to his place to dance and sing. It was party hardy with the pettifogger. Merrymount wasn't a colony; it was a night club. Thomas had been a Crown lawyer in England and now was just enjoying life in the amazing new world.

The priggish Pilgrims in Plymouth heard about Morton's one-man heathen festival in Quincy and became infuriated. The nerve of anyone to have fun! They sent out the Pilgrim Police to arrest Morton and bring him back for public Plymouth punishment. Poor Tom Morton actually stood in stocks in Plymouth for 10 days for not being a boring religious dolt, for having fun, and for loving and trusting his Red brothers and sisters.

The date of 1642 is approximate.

4

George Washington's Momma Saves the Country

There was a popular comic strip that debuted in the early 1970's called "Momma" in which Momma is always laying the guilt trip on the son. Funny stuff. But did you know that George Washington's mom saved the country by putting the guilt trip on her son George?

In 1751, an 18-year old boy named George Washington could not tell a lie. He told his mother that he wanted to go off and join the Royal Navy. Lawrence Washington, George's older brother, had gone off to sail the seven seas in the Royal Navy and George really worshipped the older boy. When Lawrence came home on leave, his stories of adventure from battles in the Caribbean made George dream of joining up to follow him.

At the age of 18, George was ready to go. The carriage was on its way to pick him up and take him off to a new life as a sailor in the Royal Navy. His bags were packed at the threshold. The carriage driver called his name. When he tried to say good-bye to his mother she gave him the works:

"Go ahead George, leave me alone with no one to look after me.

"Just go ahead and have fun. Think of yourself first, just like all my children do.

"Don't worry about me. I'll be fine with no one here to help around the house, my two boys in some faraway place, having a great time."

George put his bags down, took a deep breath and said:

"Okay Mama, you win."

George paid the driver to be on his way without him and the rest is history.

Who knows what would have become of the United States of America if George Washington had joined the navy. His brother Lawrence died of disease in the Caribbean, and a similar fate might have awaited Little George. The mother of the father of our country saved the day.

Thomas Flexner wrote a biography of Washington called *The Indispensable Man*, which is where this story comes from. The book's title is accurate.

5
<u>Newburgh Conspiracy - 1783</u>

Washington's bad eyesight saved the United States of America in 1783.

The officers of the old Continental Army stationed in Newburgh, NY were in an understandably foul mood because they hadn't been paid in a while. I can only imagine how they felt. I've made countless calls to comedy booking agents for being a month late on a paycheck from Goof-ball's Comedy Cave. I was doing stand-up comedy. These poor guys had risked their lives in combat, given up their life at home and had won a revolution for millions of others who had risked nothing. And these patriots hadn't been paid in *years.*

The angry unpaid officers had a lot of meetings, and more or less decided they were going to march on Congress to stage a military revolt. If they had to destroy the gains of the revolution to make sure they got paid, that's what they would do then. If they had to set up a temporary military dictatorship to make sure they got paid, that's what they would do then.

Washington heard all the awful rumors and called for a grand meeting of all the disgruntled officers. Washington gave a long talk about how we all had to hang in there and be patient and that it was wrong to overreact and throw away all we had gained over mere money. He used the word 'we' a few times, but it had no impact. The men just stared angrily at him no matter what he said. Washington was beaten and broken. He knew there was no placating these angry men and he knew it was hard to blame them. After all, Washington was a rich man and most of his officers were not.

They didn't budge an inch and told him that if he would not lead them in their demands, they would march on New York City without him.

Finally, Washington gave up and said he had one last prepared statement to read to them. He took some paper out of his pocket and struggled to read it. He couldn't get past two sentences before he stopped and had to dig into his coat for his reading glasses. Washington was embarrassed. The proud man had never worn his glasses in front of anyone before. No one else knew he used them, except his wife.

As he was fumbling with the papers, he humbly started to explain that he had given so many years to the cause of liberty and independence that, "somewhere along the way, I have grown old." Now his eyesight was failing him and he couldn't read a simple piece of paper anymore.

He apologized for his poor performance in trying to read his statement. He started to resume reading the paper, but at this point the content of the paper no longer mattered. What mattered was that Washington was breaking their hearts in revealing his physical weakness. They had always looked up to him as a nearly perfect hero, and they were not ready for this one. How could they defy him now?

As he fumbled trying to read the statement through his old-guy glasses, the men melted. A few began to shed tears, and then a few more. The whole angry officer corps broke down and wept. They felt their shame for defying this great guy. In exposing his frail eyes, Washington had opened theirs. The Newburgh Conspiracy melted away in a sea of tears and love for George Washington.

6
"Destroy the Letter C!"

The burning of Washington, D.C. in 1814 - perhaps the low point of American military history - was a punitive excursion, not a large theatre invasion with intent to annex or occupy.

The USA had started this uncivilized behavior at Toronto (or York, as it was known at the time) a year before. Many American history books conveniently omit this little detail; that Americans had set fire to all Canadian government buildings in Toronto in an act of wanton violence and that the burning of Washington was a direct retaliation for this.

Although the USA managed to defend Baltimore (the battle that inspired Francis Scott Key to write the Star Spangled Banner), the Royal punitive excursion in the Chesapeake of August 14 was a strategic success for England. The American nation was definitely chastised. You eat the President's dinner, then burn his house down; that sends a definite message.

But at dusk on the night Washington burned, a tornado touched down and put the fires out! The only reason that is not a famous story is that the next morning, the leader of the punitive expedition - the arrogant scoundrel Admiral Cockburn - made sure the government buildings saved by the tornado were set afire all over again and finished off. Otherwise, the miracle tornado would have made for a legend to celebrate forever, like the divine wind that once won a naval war for Japan

Crusty Cockburn had it in for the *Washington Intelligencer*, a paper even more biased and slanted than today's *New York Times!*

The *Intelligencer* wrote a lot of negative things about the invaders, and particularly about their generals. Cockburn had been reading intelligent, biting articles about himself for weeks, and now he could finally get his hands on the pen-pushing flounders at the *WI*. Cockburn had the *Washington Intelligencer* set on fire even before he burned the White House. He had his priorities. His men dismantled and demolished the printing presses as Cockburn watched with glee and actually yelled:

"Boys, be extra sure you smash in all the C's! This rag will never slander my name again!"

Talk about a guy who couldn't handle bad reviews. He was more vindictive than Harry Truman. Cockburn was like Liberty Valance when he read the negative review of his act in the *Shinbone Star*.

7
Petticoat Peggy Eaton Puts Van Buren in the White House

Andrew Jackson couldn't seem to avoid trouble with women, no matter how innocent his own behavior. Which brings us to the infamous Peggy Eaton story.

Jackson's campaign manager was J. H. Eaton, who later became Secretary of War.

Mr. Eaton had been intimate with a certain tavern owner's daughter by the name of Peggy O'Neal. Pretty Peggy had a reputation at the tavern for entertaining many a man on a stormy night. Even more so in good weather. Worse, Peggy was married to a man at sea.

This was all hearsay. No one has ever proved that Peggy entertained every other coachman who ordered a glass of double rum at her father's tavern. For all we know she might have only been very flirty and outgoing and nothing more. But if the gossipers of 1829 say you're a tramp, you're in trouble. Defending a charge means that you're already 49% convicted. At least that was so in 1829. One thing is likely; were she in present time, she would probably have her own reality show.

Shortly after Jackson took over the White House Peggy O'Neal's sailor husband died, freeing Peggy to be all she could be. At Jackson's insistence, J. H. Eaton quickly married his now single lady.

Polite society of Washington politics decided, nevertheless, but not surprisingly, to shun the newly minted Mrs. Eaton like a plague. When Peggy and John walked onto a ballroom floor they were soon dancing alone. The wives of the other cabinet members (especially Mrs. John Calhoun, the Veep's wife) refused to even speak to poor Peg. By today's standards her behavior probably wasn't particularly shameful, but by the rules of 1829 she was a bad girl.

Jackson was furious with his henpecked cabinet members who could not control their holier-than-thou wives. When Miss Donelson - the hostess of the White

House and the President's niece - joined the social boycott of Mrs. Eaton, Jackson sent his hostess cupcake home to Tennessee.

Andrew was especially intolerant of all this moral condescension partly because he was still steamed about the unfair scandalous whisperings that had once been spread about his own dear wife, Rachel.

Secretary of State Martin Van Buren, on the other hand, was a widower and he had no trouble treating Mrs. Eaton with every courtesy. Van Buren went one better. He devised a plan to get Jackson out of the Peggy mess, a scheme for a complete shake-up of the cabinet that would remove Secretary of War Eaton and with him, his troublesome wife. Van Buren would resign first, so that when Jackson ordered a shake-up, it would appear to have been triggered by the resignation of his Secretary of State, not because of his burdensome Secretary of War.

VB's plan worked. Van Buren resigned as Secretary of State. Other cabinet members were dismissed and in the middle of all the political battle-smoke, Secretary of War Eaton quietly resigned. The stupid Peggy Eaton scandal was over.

Van Buren's behavior got him on Jackson's good side and, combined with Jackson's falling out with Calhoun over 'Nullification,' led to Van Buren's supplanting Calhoun as the heir apparent to King Andrew's throne. Van Buren would replace Calhoun as the VP candidate for 1832. Van Buren also helped his own cause, because Jackson had publicly declared that he did not want Presidential candidates in his cabinet (the Jefferson in the John Adams cabinet precedent worried him). If "Matty," as Jackson called him, wanted to be the successor, he had to get out of the cabinet first; and he did. To this day the VP may sit in on many important cabinet meetings, but is not technically a member of the POTUS Cabinet.

The Peggy Eaton affair became commonly known as "The Petticoat War." It was the subject of a major movie in 1933 titled *The Gorgeous Hussy,* starring Joan Crawford as Peggy O'Neal Eaton. I haven't seen it so I can't rip it, but Minister to Russia John Randolph gets assassinated in the movie for some reason. Obviously he did not in real life. Jackson's romance with his wife Rachel was also made into a 1966 movie called *"The President's Lady,"* starring Charlton Heston as Andrew Jackson and a stunning Irene Ryan as Rachel.

8
Angelina Grimke Addresses the Massachusetts State Legislature

In the world of 1837 show business (otherwise known at the time as 'the church'), there was a major national tour by two traveling minstrels named Sarah and Angelina Grimke. These two women were daughters of South Carolina slaveholders. The Grimke sisters hated slavery. These courageous women defied their parents, who loved slavery.

South Carolina cast Sarah and Angelina out of the state for speaking out courageously against evil...I mean slavery. I always get those two mixed up.

The sisters fled north. The Grimke sisters published influential tracts and in 1837 went on a SRO (standing room only) speaking tour of the churches of the North. They were truly preaching to the choir, while in the South they were persona non grata. If Sarah and Angie had been men, their lives would have been in danger wherever they roamed. Old fashioned mores came in handy for many female abolitionists. Women often led the Abolitionists crusader events, because the racist men were hamstrung by their own too-conservative value system that forbade violence against women, at least not by a gentleman. How could they solve a problem like Angelina?

"Cain't beat her up, cain't kill her? Now what we do? Dang!"

On their tour, Sarah and Angelina not only spoke against slavery, they demanded equality for women in general; black and white. They were 'two-for-one' reformers. The Grimkes claimed that the white women in the North had a special bond with black slave females in the South. The Grimkes blended abolitionism and feminism into one batter.

Grimkeism caused a rift within the abolitionist movement. Some Abbies wanted the issue of abolitionism to be the beginning and the end of the movement. Even those who agreed with tag-along causes like women's rights, free education and care for the insane often felt that the chance for success in any issue would be reduced by an attempt to win several at once.

In 1838, Angelina became the first woman ever to address an elected assembly in the United States. Garrulous Grimke lectured the Massachusetts Legislature on the twin evils of slavery and the doctrine of male supremacy. Her stories of conditions in the South, as she had witnessed with her own eyes, moved many. The Speaker of the House was crying for half the speech.

Angelina was the first person to speak to these people about slavery from having seen it in person. When she was five years old she saw a slave whipped and she went inside crying. By the time she was 13, Angie Grimke was sneaking into the slave huts and teaching them to read and write. She nursed the wounds of the whipped.

Angie Grimke married the famous abolitionist Theodore Dwight Weld on May 14, 1838 in Philadelphia. The ceremony and the service were performed without a minister. Pennsylvania law allowed anyone to perform a legal marriage as long as there were 12 witnesses. Mr. Abolitionist Himself, Mr. William Garrison, married the liberal lovebirds.

Teddy Weld inserted a statement into the service about the injustice of too much power being vested in husbands. He condemned the idea that a bride is supposed to "obey." TD Weld said in his prepared statement that a husband has no right over the property or the person of his wife.

"She is not welded to anyone," said Weld.

And where did the Abbies go for their Honeymoon? Ocho Rios, Jamaica? No, that was me. Las Vegas? No. Wasn't built yet. Angelina and Ted rode off to a meeting of the Antislavery Convention on the other side of town.

The Grimke sisters, to the last years of their lives, continued to fight for women's rights. Angelina and Sarah often tried to register to vote in places where it was forbidden for females.

The Grimke Sisters rock. They are not as famous as they should be. I hope they at least have the Medal of Freedom. They can put them on currency as far as I'm concerned.

9
<u>The Knit-Wit of Ipswich</u>

In 1836, a woman in Ipswich, MA decided she had heard enough of her preacher every Sunday giving speeches that included a defense of slavery. Mrs. Almira Sweet was an expert practitioner of passive-aggression.

Sweet was fond of knitting. She went to church one Sunday, sat in the front row for the vermin sermon, and caused a minor row by knitting as loud as could be. Her clicking needles disrupted the preacher's preachings over and over. Minister Noonan stopped the sermon many times asking her to "desist." The next Sunday, Sweetie was up to her knitting tricks again. Noonan stopped and told her angrily to "knock it off!" as the crowd gasped.

By the third Sunday the authorities were waiting for Almira. As soon as she began knitting, Almira was arrested and removed from the Ipswich Church!

Pastor Noonan told the crowd:

"It's about time we did something about the Knit-wit of Ipswich."

The congregation applauded and laughed. Sweet was expelled like a hobo from an LA park, and was taken to Shirley Correctional Institute. But the jailer took the Sweet side and set her free immediately. He said the church had no right to order the arrest of anyone. Three cheers for that guy!

The Sweet knit-wit case got some publicity, and soon the knitting thing caught on. Knitting loudly became a badge of honor for defiant youth. Boston girls began going to dozens of churches of pro-slavery ministers; armed with their knitting needles, disrupting sermons as a group. They knitted shawls that read:

"May the points of our needles prick the slaveholders' consciences!"

All this comes from the book, *The Bold Brahmins*, by Lader; and I have to tell you that the Internet has nothing on this knitting story. Nothing. Even the Ipswich Historical Society has nothing on this. Not on their website, anyway.

Proving   indisputably   that   people   who   say,

"everything's on the Internet now, so there's no need for books," are a bunch of nit-wits too.

10
I Am Not An Actor – Tyler Demands to be Sworn In

Many people were angry with Vice President John Tyler of Virginia for assuming the title of President after the death of President William Henry Harrison in 1841. John received many death threats in the mail.

Why were these people so mad at Tyler?

It was understood that upon the death of a president, the vice president would assume the duties of president. But, it was not understood that he would take the full title of President. Some felt that a president should be elected, and that the title should thusly be earned. The Constitution, after all, only states that the _duties_ would devolve on the VP. It says nothing about swearing in the VP as the new President.

But John Tyler refused to perform under the title of "Acting President." John demanded that he be officially and ceremoniously sworn in, or else he would not so much as sign a single piece of legislature of any kind. The baby got his way. Congress recognized him officially as "President Tyler." The system of the Vice President becoming President is based on the Tyler precedent. It could easily have gone the other way.

Tyler retained the Harrison cabinet but lost his cool when these dogs tried to limit his power. They tried to float the idea that all of the President's decisions would be put to a majority vote by the cabinet. Tyler told them off. From then on, whether or not they supported him, they knew that he was the Prez.

11
The Whig Party Ran Hot and Cold – 1840 & 1848

The following sentence should help you to remember who the two elected Whig Presidents were: William Henry Harrison died from exposure from the cold in 1841, and then in 1848, Whig Zachary Taylor spent a long afternoon in the 4th of July sun and died from that.

John Tyler and Millard 'the fill-in' Fillmore were unelected Whigs. Both were WINO's: Whigs in Name Only. President Fillmore was a cafeteria Whig; he applied some of their policies while rejecting others. The Whig Party actually expelled President Tyler from the Party while he was in office. That's how much of a dependable Whig he was. Tyler spent the last two years in office partyless.

12
The Princeton and the Peacemaker – February 28, 1844

One of the most explosive incidents in American History took place on a bright sunny winter day in February of 1844 onboard the USS warship, the *Princeton.*

Princeton took an excursion down the Potomac with a stellar guest list that included President Tyler, Secretary of State William P. Upshur, Secretary of the Navy Thomas Gilmer, several members of Congress, and the elderly, yet still hot, former First Lady Dolly Madison.

Onboard *Princeton* was a newly developed weapon of mass destruction; a 12-inch barreled cannon called "the Peacemaker." This cannon fired a 235-pound ball. By the standards of the era, it was a nuke. In fact the whole point of the excursion was to show off to the gilded guests this 'peace through strength' monster gun. Peacemaker demonstrated its prowess with several astounding shots throughout the trip as the celebrities oohed and aahed. It flattened some old buildings alongside the river with impressive efficiency. Peacemaker got several rounds of applause.

The *Princeton* cruised downriver and then turned back towards Washington. Peacemaker was loaded up for one final, extra impressive shot. Just then President Tyler was called below to speak with someone. This saved his life.

Peacemaker's next shot was its last. It was a terrible misfire. The explosion blew the ship half out of the water and killed 12 people!

Peacemaker became the piece-maker, cutting several peaceful people to pieces on the *Princeton.* The dead included the American Secretary of State, the Secretary of War and a United States Senator! A Mr. Gardner, who was scheduled to become Tyler's son-in-law, also died.

The Peacemaker changed history because Calhoun, the new Secretary of State, had some ideas about foreign policy that were different from the dear departed Upshur. Especially on the Texas issue. The Peacemaker inadvertently helped trigger the Mexican War. Calhoun did not want to even become Secretary of State but he took the job just so he could help get Texas for the USA.

Senator Thomas H. Benton of Missouri was knocked almost unconscious by the peacemaker blast. Andrew Jackson later said he believed that the explosion had affected Benton's mind. And when Andy Jackson says that you're soft as a grape, you know you've got problems.

13
<u>Beverly Williams - 1847</u>

Beverly Williams was a young black man who wanted to enroll at Harvard University for the fall semester of 1847. He was qualified and passed all his entrance exams. But when word got out regarding the man about to enter the hallowed halls of Harvard, the true color of the university came out - and it wasn't crimson.

White students and pale-faced locals organized protests against the admission of a black to the great place of liberal learning. Harvard had kicked Emerson out for questioning the miracles of the Bible earlier in the decade, and once again the school was getting poor grades on progressivism.

But Beverly Williams had a champion in the person of Edward Everett. The famous Massachusetts statesman was now the President of Harvard. Everett announced:

"If I have to expel every student and keep this University open just to educate one man, by God I will do so."

A showdown was coming. Would Everett really keep Harvard open just to educate one man of color?

Beverly Williams solved the jam by getting a bad case of tuberculosis and dying right around the time he should have been starting classes. What a shame. Harvard waited 23 more years before admitting an African-American. If Beverly had not become ill, a great national spotlight might have hit the Cambridge controversy of 1847 and changed the course of American civil rights history, resulting in who knows what cause and effect consequences on so many other events.

14
<u>Box Brown – March 23-24, 1849</u>

One of the greatest stories ever is of a slave who had himself mailed to freedom from Virginia to Philadelphia in a box! It's that simple. He mailed himself free!

The slave was a great guy named Charles Johnson, but he has come down to history named after the packing crate that freed him. "Box Brown" conspired with a white doctor in Philadelphia named Kenny McKim to escape slavery in Richmond by using the U.S. postal service.

The box was only three feet long, two feet deep, and two feet wide. CJ's fellow slaves hammered the box shut and dragged him to the post office for delivery to Doc McKim. The unwitting enabler was the Adams Express Shipping Corporation of Richmond.

The trip covered 350 miles and took 28 hours. At one stretch, Charlie in the box was upside down for three hours next to some chatty passengers on a ferry. He wanted to turn around, but did not dare move. Brown later said he almost passed out at this point. Doctor McKim later said that during this stretch Brown was probably flirting with death.

When the "box" was delivered to Dr. McKim he opened it in front of a group of freedom's friends. Up popped Brown with a grin and said with a near shout:

"Good morning gentlemen!"

Everyone cheered. Johnson stood up and smiled again, but then fainted. It had been a long trip.

Many Abbies wanted to tell the story far and wide, but the true friends of freedom knew that to tell the story would ruin the chance for some other slaves trying the same gag. In spite of urgings to "ixne," the story got around and sure enough Adams Express caught two slaves trying to mail themselves to Elmira NY. Adams told their workers at the company to always tap twice on the boxes and say, "knock, knock." If anyone was fool enough to reflexively respond, "who's there?" the game was up and they had to go back to slavery.

Box Johnson moved to Boston as soon as he could find

a stage-coach headed that way. By his standards, anything was a luxury mode of travel. Charles wanted to get as far away from the Mason Dixon line as possible, and, back then, Boston was famous for being *against* racism.

Brown began telling his story all over Boston and became one of the city's most popular citizens.

When Congress passed the Fugitive Slave Law in 1850, Brown decided it was better safe than sorry, so he caught a ship to England and stayed there until Lee surrendered and it was safe to come back.

Brown became a show biz attraction for the rest of his years, telling his story with props and panoramic illustrations for dazzled audiences.

I admire Box. I can't handle the cramped airline seats on my five-and-a-half hour flight to Vegas. What a great guy. The great deed makes the great person.

15
<u>Riot at the Astor Place Opera House</u>
<u>– May 10, 1849</u>

Now here is the story about an 1849 riot in New York City in which 32 people died.

And what caused the riot? Was it food shortages?

No.

Resistance to the draft?

No.

Maybe it was a workers' strike that got out of control?

No.

Race?

No.

Nativists gone mad?

Still, no.

No, the riot that killed 32 people on May 10, 1849 was over which stage actor was better qualified to play Macbeth, the American star or the British star.

Not kidding.

The American superstar actor was Edwin Forrest and the British celebrity hambone was William C. Macready.

The trouble started when Forrest attended a performance of Hamlet in Edinburgh, Scotland. The American prima donna did not like the way Macready was interpreting the role and began hissing from the audience. Eddie kept hiss-rupting the show until others in the crowd urged Forrest to leave, which he did (without a refund).

The story got around in the states.

In May of 1849, the two actors happened to be playing Macbeth at the same time in separate venues in New York City. On May 9, 1849, a crowd of Forrest fans went to the Macready performance at the Astor Theatre for the sole purpose of disrupting the show. They pelted the stage with objects, coupled with catcalls for Macready to get off the stage. Having personally experienced similar audiences during my 40-year career as a stand-up comedian, I can tell you it is not pleasant.

The disruption was well planned. It started on cue 40

minutes into the show when one planted heckler rose and shouted, "Hey what time does the entertainment come on?" That was the cue for more heckling. Forrest fanatics then began hurling glass ashtrays and other objects at the stage. The actors finished the performance in spite of the attack.

Thuggy fans of U.S. Forrest warned UK Macready after the show that he would be taking the stage at his own risk from there on in, as far as Manhattan was concerned.

Macready was ready to quit, but Herman Melville and other local literary giants convinced him that the show must go on. "Don't give in to these uncouth squids," Melville told Macready. But this was bad advice, and by listening to Melville, Macready ended up in a whale of a jam. Forrest supporters were by then determined to physically stop the next showing of *Macbeth* at the Opera House.

On May 10, 1849 a crowd of 20,000 cultural jingoists gathered both inside and around The Astor Place Opera House. As soon as Macready began his performance Forrest's fans pelted the poor bloke with rotten eggs, potatoes, stale cupcakes, old shoes, anvils, and other objects (the Astor Theatre had judiciously discontinued placing glass ashtrays everywhere). Macready walked to the front of the stage and; dodging the tomatoes, inkwells, and cucumbers, boldly declared that he was being paid to do a job and was legally obliged to continue.

But the situation got worse. From the balcony, stones and chunks of plaster crashed down upon the actors and even upon many members of the audience. People were getting hurt. At the same time the crowd outside was getting out of control, attacking the police and throwing bricks through the windows of the theatre.

The National Guard was called out - not to protect the actors or even stop the riot, but simply to save the lives of the police. The Guardsmen battled their way through the mob and made a protective cordon around the building. There was gunfire. When the riot ended after several hours of violence, 32 people were dead. Not over an unjust war, but rather over a show business argument not worthy today of a paragraph in a second-rate tabloid.

How could this have even happened? In 1849 there weren't 22,000 celebrities, 2,400 TV shows and 1,550 movies to pick from. In 1849 the entire focus of the U.S. public was locked in on this one stupid rivalry between these two useless actors. That massive river of show business that still grips the nation today was all zeroed in on one spot in New York City and on this rivalry. There was no diversification and dispersal of show biz energy. It was all there at the Astor Opera House.

And all over Shakespeare. That mob of rabid critics made the Friday late show crowd I tried to entertain last week in Atlantic City look like a bunch of girl scouts.

Masters murdered slaves every day in the South with impunity. Women couldn't vote. Workers lived in dangerous conditions and had no rights. Who cares? But let a British actor bring his lame interpretation of *Macbeth* to a New York stage and a riot of righteousness breaks out in which 32 people died and over 100 were injured.

16
<u>Tony Burns - 1854</u>

In February of 1854, a slave named Anthony Burns escaped from Virginia and made his way North to Boston, the center of Abolitionist strength.

Burns was apprehended in Beantown in May under the barbaric Fugitive Slave Law. Soon there was excitement in the city over the fate of Mr. Burns, a buzz unlike anything seen in Boston since the Revolutionary War.

Richard Henry Dana, the famous literary figure and lawyer, interviewed the celebrity prisoner in his cell and found Tony timid, scared, confused and very much injured. Tony had a big ugly brand on one cheek. He had a broken hand; with a protruding bone to prove it.

Burns only wanted to surrender as humbly as possible to his former master Colonel Suttle, who was present during the interview between Dana and Burns. Burns felt that he was already going to be severely punished when he returned to Virginia and did not wish to futilely resist his extradition, thereby making his punishment all the worse when the appeal failed. Dana pleaded with Burns and the court for a delay of at least two days before any legal decision was made. The delay was granted.

The next day Boston was alive with talk about a possible mob rescue of Burns - sort of the reverse of the Klan sallying forth to bust a black man out of prison to lynch him.

On the sixth of May a large angry meeting at Faneuil Hall addressed the Burns crisis. Even the 'Compromise men of 1850' supported the movement to "Free Tony B." Conservatives as well as Abolitionists demanded the release of Burns, and in effect were demanding the repeal of the Fugitive Slave Law. After the meeting broke up the mob marched down to the courthouse and tried to free Tony Burns by force.

The vanguard of rabble broke in the outer door and entered the building. There, several of their number were wounded. On the other side, one official was killed; a Mr. Batchelder, who had in recent weeks been assisting in the capture of several fugitive slaves and was a known mark for the crowd.

The crazy vanguard retreated outside where they found that the big crowd had deserted them upon hearing sounds of the battle inside. Tony Burns would not be freed that night.

Reverend T. W. Higginson of Worcester was one of the men who led the attack on the courthouse.

A local doctor immediately offered to lead 200 men to re-storm the courthouse. But after the first assault, the marshals had called out the military. The building was secured with volunteer militia, marines from Charlestown, and some cannon from Fort Independence in Boston harbor. Tony was now "safe" and the trial could begin.

Wealthy abolitionists bankrolled quality lawyers for Anthony. The Burns trial gripped the city in the last days of May 1854. More than a hundred of the despised 'Marshal's Guard,' the army of federal fugitive slave catchers, sat in the courtroom with loaded revolvers at the ready.

Outside the building, huge crowds gathered during the trial. Armed soldiers with fixed bayonets had to charge the crowd more than once to teach it to keep a distance. When Colonel Suttle, the slave-owner in pursuit of Burns, went in or out of the courtroom he needed a special guard of Southern men to protect him.

On June 2, 1854 the verdict was reached. Tony Burns was guilty of being positively identified as Tony Burns. A revenue cutter was waiting at the docks to sail him back to Virginia.

"He looked the image of despair," wrote Dana.

His lawyers tried to cheer him up by telling Anthony that he was just being used as a symbol for southern pride. He wasn't going to be much of a worker with a severely broken hand. They promised they would buy his freedom as soon as he was back in the South.

To get the prisoner the short distance from the corner of State Street and Court Street to Long Wharf, 1,700 armed troops were needed to clear a path through the jeering and hissing mob of mad New Englanders. The commander of the slave-catchers, General Edmunds drew a line on both sides of the path to the cutter and ordered his troops to shoot right into the crowd if it crossed these lines anywhere along the route.

There was a tense moment when a unit saw a commotion and cocked their rifles to fire. They were just barely persuaded to desist from this re-enactment of the Boston Massacre of 1770. If they had fired into the crowd it would have happened within a thousand feet of that 1770 site, and could have had similar incendiary consequences.

When Burns was taken out of the building, troops with swords and revolvers at the ready formed a square around him, and a cannon followed behind the moving square. The marshals looked trigger happy and very nervous as they made their way to the dock while the crowd chanted, "Shame! Shame! Shame!"

A few groups of civilians were seen applauding the troops in racist support, but they were the minority. The mob was overwhelmingly with Burns, against Suttle, and was a living reflection of the Northern side of the coming Civil War. It didn't matter if some of them wore bonnets or were elderly men. These civilians in this scene were a part of the coming conflict.

Anthony Burns sailed back to Virginia in chains. His Northern friends bought his freedom in 1855. Tony died in Canada in 1862.

17
Congress Buys a Pack of Camels – March 1855

The 1855 Congress agreed to spend $30,000 to enlist camels in the U.S. Army. The plan was sponsored by Senator Harmon Filters of Mississippi. It was called the *Camel Filters Act of 1855.*

The idea was to use these humpties in the arid U.S. Southwest, a region that would remind the animals of home.

A second lieutenant first took the idea over the hump, and then Secretary of War Jefferson Davis came on board and became a spokesman for the camel cause. Horses and mules had less durability than camels in the American Sudan. Horses had to be shoed, camels didn't. Camels could eat the most useless dry shrubs that other animals would not touch in their hungriest hour. Camels, if they had to, would even eat the food at the Tropicana Hotel employees' cafeteria!

An American ship was sent to the Middle East to go buy a pack of camels. The USS *Invisible* docked in Cairo and went camel shopping. I can only surmise that they found a store with a sign reading, "Today's Special - Buy 25 Camels, Get Five Camels Free!" Whether they procured such a thrifty deal or not, the fact is that The *Invisible* returned to New York with 30 camels ready for basic training in the U.S. Army. In 1856, 41 more camels were added to the ranks of American fighting forces.

The few, the proud, the camels.

The first USACC (United States Army Camel Company) squad trotted out into New Mexico in 1856. There were subsequently a few other test expeditions in various places around the southwest.

The camels performed well, but they weren't very likable. They smelled worse than a mule, a horse, and a New York City wino combined. People would try to be nice to them and the animals (camels) would kick and bite. Sure, they did a yeocamel's job, but no one liked to work with them. They weren't engaging. The camels didn't wag their tail and fetch the ball. They were often truculent - and now you have to look up that word.

During the Civil War the camel companies were put on hold. The experiment was deserted and it faded away into the desert sunset.

Along the way, many camels were either released into the wild or escaped into the wild. History Professor Herman Hattaway says that someone let a herd of them out deliberately, and that's why the experiment was discontinued. These wild camels roamed over the American southwest for almost a hundred years, until the eve of World War II, when the last of them died out.

There is an American legend, based on a true story, and it was featured on the TV Show *"Death Valley Days"* hosted by Ronald Reagan. A strange, big animal was terrorizing a frontier California community early in the 20th Century. The monster had killed two people and injured several others. It was strange, it was a legend and it was a terror.

A gang of settlers finally tracked down this western Loch Ness Monster and sent it down in a hail of bullets like Clyde Darrow. When the rubes examined the body they realized at last what sci-fi creature had been stalking the village. It was one of those wild camels from the Camel Corps, one of the lone survivors of an experiment that went bad in 1855. This individual had apparently gone berserk and started stalking and killing humans. Camels are gnarly enough on their best days, but this one had been left alone, unloved and hungry too long, and made a decision on who was going to pay.

During the Korean War, a Turkish brigade arrived in early 1951 to help the UN. It included a small pack of camels, and a few of them got loose and roamed the Korean countryside in the middle of that war. That's all the information I have on the immigrant Korean camels. Since Korea sells dog-meat to humans in restaurants to this very day, I'd rather not speculate on what happened to those loose camels in Korea. I'm guessing they never got to see the lights of Ankara again. Poor things.

18
<u>Ann Coleman</u>

First the legend.

President James Buchanan was the only bachelor President. But he was no swinging bachelor. Jimmy's heart was broken forever by the tragic engagement to one Ann Coleman back in 1819.

Buchanan was a young man without much money, while Ann Coleman was the daughter of Robert Coleman, the wealthiest man in Lancaster County, Pennsylvania. During the engagement, James was away for a while and he wrote her letters of love every day. Ann's mother intercepted and burned those letters, while telling her daughter that James obviously didn't love her. Both parents thought that James Buchanan was not good enough for her and that he only wanted to marry her for money. They forced Ann to write James a letter breaking the engagement and telling him to never show his smug face there ever again.

When James got the letter he was crestfallen. He could not understand why she would break it off. They both knew they loved each other.

A few days later James got the worst letter of all time. This one said that Ann Coleman had committed suicide. A broken James tried to go to the funeral, but the parents blocked him from setting foot inside the church.

"Happiness has fled me forever," Buchanan wrote. And James never got real close to anyone ever again. He wasn't going to let anyone hurt him again like that a second time.

When James Buchanan became President of the United States, a very old man showed up at the White House. It was Ann Coleman's father who wanted to apologize. President Buchanan slammed the door in his face and told the guards to rough him up a bit on the way out.

God, how I wish that story was true, because it certainly works for me.

But the real story is a bit different.

The two were engaged, but "Jimbo" Buchanan was a fairly successful young lawyer. He was hardly poor. And there is no proof the Robert Coleman ever did anything to block James from courting his daughter, but he probably did, since he had a bad attitude towards any man who courted his daughter. That's why AC was still single at 23, an old maid by 1819 standards. Ann's mother never burned his love letters.

Ann, in fact, was annoyed with James for paying too much attention to his career and too little to their engagement. She wrote him some unhappy letters. She was a troubled soul, wondering if he really loved her as he claimed.

One day, when he was on his 3-day journey back home to visit Ann, he stopped by a friend's house where there was a young single girl also staying there. Nothing happened between James and the single girl, but one of Ann's gossiping friends ran back to tell Ann that James had stopped to see some other girl, and hadn't seemed to be in a hurry to rush home to see Ann.

In a jealous rage, Ann wrote a Dear John letter to Jim. It was over. Jim was shocked to read the letter. She told him that he was just a gold-digger and she never wanted to see him again.

Ann was a depressed unstable wreck after breaking up with Jim. On her mother's advice she took off on a rest and relaxation visit to her sister in Philadelphia.

On the night of December 8-9, 1819, Ann Coleman went into physical convulsions that lasted throughout the night, and died. Doctors thought she had died from symptoms brought on by hysteria. They had given her some laudanum for her hysteria, and she may actually have overdosed on that. So it may have been a suicide, an accidental overdose, or a bad reaction to a sedative. It also might have been a natural death from hysteria.

James Buchanan was truly devastated. But Buchanan had been a workaholic before he met Ann Coleman, so buried her and himself in his work, and any idea that he became married to politics because he never got over this tragedy is shaky. Jimmy's extreme dedication to his work is what had started her on her jealousy road to begin with.

The story about old man Coleman visiting the White House can't be true, because by the time Jimbo got in, the father had been dead for 30 years.

19

Simon Bolivar Buckner – and Son

The loser at Fort Donelson, and the first Southern general to surrender a Confederate Army in the Civil War, Simon B. Buckner, is not exactly a candidate to become the fourth man on Stone Mountain.

Buckner really dropped the ball when he surrendered Fort Donelson to Grant in February of 1862. Simon B. became a prisoner of war, but was exchanged and went back onto the battlefield later in the war.

After the war, Buckner went into politics and became the Governor of Kentucky from 1887 to 1891. A Democrat, of course.

His son was killed in action in 1945 on Okinawa! Yes, his son. Do the math. That's hard to believe, but it's true.

The Rebel general lived a long life and had a child when he was almost 60. Junior was born on June 18, 1886 and had a long military career. General Simon Bolivar Buckner, Jr. died in combat on Okinawa in 1945. That's almost incredible to me.

Not only that, SBB Sr. had also served in the Mexican War. So an officer who served in the Mexican War had a son who was killed in 1945 on Okinawa.

20
Jack Ass at Glorietta Pass – February 1862

Just before the Battle at Glorietta Pass in the upper Rio Grande in February 1862, the Union tried a wild and deadly "Trojan Donkey" trick on the Confederates. Union men packed two mules with 80 pounds of explosives each, then snuck up close to the Rebel line late at night and pushed the poor animals off towards the Rebs with slow fuses burning in their packs.

The mules took a few steps towards the Confederate position, but then stopped when they realized that the Union men were walking the other way. The humans that had been feeding them for months were their buddies. The mules turned and began walking back the other way towards their attempted murderers as if to say, "Hey fellas, where ya goin? I thought we were friends."

The men in blue started walking faster away from the mules. The mules walked a little faster too. Then a trot. Then the mules trotted. "Hey wait for me!" they cried in donkey language with the fuses burning closer to the powder. Then the men broke into a terrified full scale run for the Rio Grande. The mules broke into a full gallop with the bombs about to go off. Dramatic music please...

The mules blew sky high just moments before they caught up with the Union troops in the Rio Grande.

That scene wrote itself. Which one of those jack asses in the Union command forgot how stubborn, and maybe even affectionate, mules are?

And remember, "the stubbornest mule stays closets to the whip."

21
<u>The Stretcher - 1862</u>

This next story of humor amidst terror happened in a battle shortly after the Second Bull Run.

Union General Pope's troops were getting the worst of it in an ongoing battle. Union troops holding their position saw a smaller force retreating out of the woods and falling back towards a clearing. The retreating Union troops were in a panic. Two soldiers in brightly colored Zouave regiment uniforms were heroically carrying a wounded man into this clearing on a stretcher. The Rebels were pressing hard. When a bomb landed near them the two brave men dropped the stretcher and just ran for daylight leaving their injured pal behind. Fellow Union troops were watching all this from entrenched positions.

The best part is yet to come.

The wounded guy jumped off the grounded stretcher and ran so fast towards the Union lines that he passed the two men, still running, who had been carrying him! Hundreds of Union troops witnessed the scene and laughed till their stomachs hurt.

22
__The Organ Grinder__

He was a hustler's hustler.

Lincoln hired a spy to go live in Richmond disguised as an organ grinder. The man had requested a meeting with Lincoln and volunteered his services in the cause with his clever original plan. He would live in Richmond as an organ grinder and keep an eye on everything said in and around the Confederate's capital building. Lincoln gave the guy money to buy a monkey and an organ, and to go live in Richmond and report back detailed military info. On completing the mission he would get a nice payoff for his bravery.

The man returned with a lot of detailed charts and maps and statistical lists. He picked up his pay plus a down payment on his second mission and off he went. But the man was eventually discovered to be a fraud. He had never been to Richmond, had never bought a monkey, and had invented all the charts and stats about the Confederate Army. And then no one could find him anywhere. He got away with it. The all-time bold hustler. The man who made a monkey out of Lincoln.

23
<u>Fireside Chat</u>

A delegation came to Lincoln in late 1862 with a paper they had drafted. Among them were businessmen, bankers, and politicians. They were there claiming that a certain Senator Ned Baker, a Republican, had been dishonest in how he handed out government jobs.

Lincoln listened to their story, took the document in his hands and then asked, "Is this mine to do with as I please?"

"Of course, Mr. President," came the reply.

Lincoln calmly walked over to the fireplace, put the papers into the fire and sat down and watched them burn. Then he stood up, looked over, gave them the famous Lincoln stare and said, "Will there be anything else, gentlemen?"

After they had slithered out, Lincoln told an aide that he had been so angry he could not speak. The gesture of burning the paper may have seemed vicious, but for Lincoln it was the only way he could successfully manage his anger. Ned Baker was an old friend of Lincoln.

In any case, I love this scene. Go Lincoln, go!

24
Doubleday – Major General Abner Doubleday – 1813-1893

Some of you dummies think Abner Doubleday invented the game of baseball. Doubleday did not invent baseball. Alexander Cartwright invented baseball. The widely accepted story that a Mr. Abner Doubleday invented baseball on a cow pasture in 1839 is a lie. In fact the man who started this legend later killed his own wife and was put in a lunatic asylum. The only evidence that Doubleday invented baseball was that single nutcake telling his tale to someone who then retold the fabrication to a baseball committee which, at that moment, was researching the origins of the game.

Abner Doubleday probably never even saw a game in his entire life. Abner never even so much as mentioned the word baseball one time, written or spoken – at least not to the best of anyone's knowledge. Abner Doubleday happened to be a student at West Point when he was supposedly inventing baseball at Cooperstown in 1839.

What Abner Doubleday did invent was the famous cable car system in steep, hilly San Francisco. It was Doubleday who made the Rice-a-Roni song possible. Doubleday held the patent for decades (on the cable cars, not the Rice-a-Roni song).

Oh, and he saved the day for the Union at Gettysburg. On the first of the three-day battle, July 1, 1863, General Doubleday led a stout defense of 8,000 men against 16,000 Rebs on the north side of the village. In hours of hard fighting, the Union fell back through the village of Gettysburg and just south of it. But this fighting retreat made everything else that followed possible. Doubleday's fighting retreat made Lee's advance through Gettysburg as slow as molasses, enabling Union reinforcements to arrive at this held position.

What a shame that some baseball fairy tale has to supersede Abner's genuinely great achievements.

Doubleday was also at Fort Sumter in April 1861 when

it surrendered to start the war. He was number two in command at Sumter and helped to fire the first return cannon shot against the CSA shore batteries.

So AD fires the first shot for the Union in the Civil War, saves the day at Gettysburg, invents the San Francisco cable car system, and his legacy is based on something he didn't even do. Too often, the worst thing that can happen to history is history. Once a version gets locked in, it's hard to change it, not matter how many myth-buster books come out.

25
<u>The Terror of Ugly Husbands</u>

Rebel General Earl Van Dorn lost at Pea Ridge (March 1862), lost at Corinth (May 1862), and then got shot by a jealous Southern husband while sitting at his desk on May 7, 1863. The murder happened at Spring Hill Tennessee, about 20 miles south of Nashville. The husband was so obviously in the right, he was never prosecuted for murder! The shooter, Dr. James Bodie Peters, had "OJ's luck."

Earl Van Dorn was a Texan and a great horseman. As a general, he was considered in the same class as talents like Jimmy (JEB) Stuart and Nat Bed Forrest. Van Dorn had served courageously in the Mexican War and in the wars with the American Indians. Van Dorn was wounded at Shiloh in 1862.

He was a man's man, but unfortunately for his longevity, a ladies man too. Too much so.

EVD was married to Caroline Gobold Van Dorn, but that didn't stop him from doing his Bill Clinton impressions. Van Dorn was as talented as he was handsome. He could paint a postcard while reciting an original poem. Maybe he was too cute for his own good.

The Dr. Carl Austin Weiss in our story is, as mentioned, Dr. James Bodie Peters. Doc Peters kept hearing rumors that his wife was involved with this world famous cad.

Van Dorn's reputation as a home-wrecker was becoming such common knowledge that a Nashville newspaper writer gave him the title "The Terror of Ugly Husbands." The locals had a good laugh, but the nickname was loaded with gunpowder. Now any man whose wife was rumored to be involved with Van Dorn had to suffer a double humiliation. Now he was not only a loser, but an ugly loser. That's where we all draw the line!

Peters sent Van Dorn a written warning that, "If you so much as set one foot on my front lawn I will personally blow your head off."

I guess he was kind of mad.

But writing the warning note only made the writer

angrier. The mad Doc set out on horseback in a race with his letter to the Martin Cheairs Mansion near Nashville, which was the local Confederate HQ. Van Dorn had an office at the Mansion.

Peters parked his horse. The guards gave him a casual hello. Peters was a familiar figure at the Mansion. He was like Jack Ruby at the garage entrance. Peters walked into Van Dorn's office. Van Dorn was sitting at his desk writing something. Peters walked up behind him and said, "Don't move. There's a pistol two inches from the back of your head. You have been having an affair with my wife. You know who I am!"

General Van Dorn, military hero, swore up and down that the intruder was mistaken (a lie). He offered to write a public letter vouching for the virtue of Mrs. Peters. Hubby Peters said, "No thanks," and shot him in the back of the head. Van Dorn died four hours later.

Peters casually left Confederate headquarters and got back on his horse with a wave goodbye to the guards. They obviously hadn't heard the shot. Peters turned himself in a couple days later.

Because Van Dorn had been warned many times before that something like this might happen, and because it was wartime and the legal system was not functioning in the South at full throttle, and because most people sympathized with the Southern honor of the shooter, James Bodie Peters was never prosecuted for murder.

I don't know if he patched things up with his wife after that, or not. What do you think?

26
Jimmy Hanger – Confederate War Hero

I don't look up to many Confederates as being "war heroes." But I will make an exception for Jimmie Hanger.

James Hanger was shot in the leg at the Battle of Philippi in 1862. The leg was amputated and Hanger went home to Georgia. Jimmy locked himself up in his room and wouldn't talk to anyone for months. He left his meal-plate outside the door and became a recluse. But he did ask for tools and wood. His family would hear him working in there on something, Lord knew what it was.

Then, one day, after three months of total isolation, James E. Hanger came walking down the stairs with his new invention, a prosthetic leg. The Hanger leg could bend at the knee and the ankle! He invented it and made it all by himself!

Hanger's leg became a national news story. Both armies, North and South, copied it. He had not only helped himself, he had given great help to masses of the afflicted.

And Hanger's leg had legs. It has lasted to the present day. The Hanger Orthopedic Group is currently worth $486 million. The Hanger family was bought out decades ago, but the name remains.

27
<u>The Shawl – April 3, 1865</u>

United States Army General Godfrey Weitzel triumphantly entered Richmond at 8:00 am on April 3, 1865.

President Lincoln was on the Potomac in the riverboat *Malvern* later that same April 3. He had surprised his aides when he said, "I'm going to Richmond." Abraham hoped that his presence in the Rebel capital might bring home the message to the entire South that the war was lost and over. Or, he just wanted to go.

Malvern plodded its way to Richmond Harbor, but got stuck in the mud, ruining Lincoln's chance to disembark like Doug MacArthur. Linc had to hop into a rowboat. Six men rowed the President, his son Tad, and a single guard to a dock at the edge of the city.

Waiting there to greet Lincoln was a small crowd of blacks. When Lincoln stepped ashore they fell to their knees and thanked him as their savior. Many had heard rumors that the end of the war meant their freedom, but this was not certain in their minds. What proof did they have that the legendary emancipator was even real? Now here he stood in the flesh telling them:

"Don't bow to me, my friends, only bow to the Lord. It is God you must thank for your freedom."

Their spokesperson replied:

"We meant no disrespect. But after so many years in the desert without water, it's a joy to be looking at the spring of life."

They got up and there stood the President, shaking hands with every black person who wished to meet him.

A short time later, a guard of 12 Union sailors formed a protective square around the Presidential party for the walk to the Rebel capitol building. Word was out, and as the party marched, the crowds grew until there was an impressive spectacle of spectators lining the streets and hanging out every window to watch Lincoln pass. The broken city just stared in silence as the square marched by. There was no cheering, and there were no abusive calls either. It would have been a piece of cake for anyone to kill Lincoln from a window, and any small gang of aggressors could have overwhelmed the small party and hacked them to bits. Some of the guards mumbled that they would feel safer if someone would yell something hateful at them. It would at least break the scary spell of the threatening silence.

There was only one sign of friendship from the Richmond people. Between a hotel and a public building was a wooden pedestrian bridge and the party had to walk under it. On the bridge stood a lone, young Southern belle. The shawl she wore on her shoulders was the flag of the United States of America. She had obviously made it herself, just waiting for the day.

28

Why Russia Sold Alaska to the United States - 1867

President Andrew Johnson gets credit for the Alaska purchase, but it was not much his doing. Andrew Johnson was not a hands-on president when it came to foreign policy. His Secretary of State, William Henry Seward, who had made a remarkable recovery from his near fatal wounding in the Lincoln assassination, had, in fact, nearly a free hand to run foreign affairs. Seward was as ardent an expansionist as James Polk or W. Bush.

Seward wanted to annex several islands in the Caribbean as well as Canada. And he wanted America to have the Hawaiian Islands too. Seward's prospects were frustrated in the Johnson era, partly from a national exhaustion due to the long Civil War.

The one notable success for this manifest hawk was Alaska.

Russia sold Alaska, because it feared it would lose it anyway in the next war with Great Britain. A cold war had been under way between them for decades, and it had erupted hot in the short, but bloody Crimean War of the 1850's (France and Britain vs. Russia).

During that war, Britain and Russia had agreed to a neutral status for Alaska, making it a distant demilitarized zone, like the USA and USSR agreeing to a demilitarization of outer space in the 1960's.

By 1867 the Lion and the Bear were at odds in Central Asia (The "Great Game") and the Tsar was not sure that England would make the same deal for Alaskan neutrality if war broke out, which seemed more probable than merely possible. The English warships were getting better all the time. Alaska might just look like an appetizing theatre of operations for a Sea Lion. Moscow deemed it better to sell Alaska to the Americans, a rival of the British, than to let the mighty English Navy grab it for free. That would have been a disaster to Tsar Al II. Instead of a limited prize of improved friendship with the USA and some dough, the loss of Alaska to Britain would also cost the Russians in prestige. This is why the price was so low and why the Russians were so eager to sell. Alaska was definitely priced to sell. Russia didn't exactly want America to have it. The sale was to ensure that Britain did not have it.

Russia's feared next war with the English never came. Russian-British relations evolved from 19th century cold war to allies in the two world wars of the 20th century. But no one knew the future in 1867 and the USA got the bargain in the bargain.

On March 30, 1867 Secretary of State Seward negotiated with Al 2. The final price was 7.2 million dollars. The Senate ratified the sale on October 18 after a difficult debate. Several fools ridiculed Alaska as being a foolish purchase. They called it "Seward's Folly" or "Seward's Icebox." Except for fishing, it was supposedly useless. Even the fur trade up there was on the decline, much of the stock having been depleted.

Near the end of the 1800's gold was discovered in the Klondike - lots of it - making Seward an overnight retroactive hero.

Mineral resources have been explored and developed throughout the 20th century and into the 21st. The Alaska pipeline sends oil south to the 48 contiguous. Alaska was, in the final analysis of course, an outstanding purchase and the people who scoffed at it in 67 go down in history as two-ounce brains.

The myth is that the Russians foolishly sold Alaska for a song to the USA, like the Indians who sold Manhattan for $24. They supposedly had no idea of the mineral wealth there and were the big chumps when the USA found gold and oil.

But, in fact, the Russians had a pretty good idea that American prospectors would find rich deposits of gold there sooner or later and when that happened there would be a gold rush followed by an expansion of manifest destiny. Better to sell now before they lost it to the insatiable American expansionism anyway. If they got into a scrap with expansionist America over Alaska, Russia would lose a key alliance in its goal of competing with and containing the British.

Russia was also quite happy to box the British in to the interior of the North America continent. Russia did not want the British navy operating from the northwest coast. With American territory to the north and west, British Columbia could never directly threaten Russia again. In the 1867 Russian mind, the UK was the big threat, not America.

Now, a sorry side to the Alaska story.

Of the 7.2 million paid, only 7 million went to the Tsar. Of the remaining 200 boxes of ziti, 136 were never accounted for. The rest went to above board expenses including legitimate consulting fees. What happened to the missing money is fairly clear but not provable. The best evidence (among much) comes from an account by President Johnson of a ride in the country he took one Sunday afternoon with his Secretary of State in 1871. The two men were going off to the country to get hammered on good whiskey. During their good time with the bottle Seward began to get loose-lipped.

"Johnny," he said (his nickname for 'Johnson'), "Did it ever cross your mind how surprisingly easy the Alaska Treaty passed the Senate? What was it, (burp) two votes against it?"

"What are you driving at, Sew?"

"Half those votes were bought and paid for by the very dough they were voting to appropriate."

"No. Stop. I've changed my mind. I don't want to hear any more," said Johnson.

"Well you're going to hear it," said Seward, with a slug of whiskey. He wanted to get it off his chest. It was like *Mr. Smith Goes to Washington* where that manly-voiced lady finally opens Mr. Smith's eyes to what a sap he's been; like John Wayne blowing smoke in Jimmy Stewart's face telling him what really happened the night Liberty Valance died.

"Surely you remember how much opposition there was to our buying Alaska. Even you weren't all for it. I was a one-man band. Then all of a sudden it passes the Senate 38-2? Come on Andy, open your eyes."

Johnson grabbed a swig, let out a burp and said, "Let's hear it."

"Thaddeus Stephens got $11,000 from Russian Minister Stoeckl for his vote, payable after the money was paid to him by the U.S. Government. Then he took some of that 11 grand and bought up the votes he needed. Stoeckl bought off a few in the Senate. And he cleaned the House."

"Are you saying that the bill never would have passed if the Russian minister hadn't greased the skids with money paid for by the very treaty appropriation they were debating?"

"In the Senate, maybe. In the House..." Seward paused and looked at Johnson and said in a low exaggerated voice, "De-fi-nite-leeee"

29
Women Get the Vote in W
1869

In 1869, Wyoming became the first state
vote to women. There was some ulterior moti
because the state desperately needed women. ⸻ales
dominated the census by a six-to-one margin and the place
had a reputation for lawlessness. The franchise for women
would hopefully attract female settlers.

Some sources tell me that this was the first time any
woman was allowed to vote in any country! In any case, the
first woman to ever vote in America was Louisa Ann
Gardner Swain who voted in Wyoming on September 6,
1870. She voted "yes" on the referendum question "Should
men make a formal apology for the past 2,000 years?"

Social progress was almost always more advanced in
the west. It was impossible to enforce Philadelphia morals
on the frontier. There was, in fact, no great protest in
Wyoming when the state proposed to let women vote. What
would have been viewed in the east as, "Well! I never!"
was viewed in the west as, "Yeah, whatever."

Colorado was next, granting women the vote in 1876,
but only in school elections. Big deal.

The American West in the 1870's was like the
American East in the 1770's, a place where people could
get away from the squares back east with their antiquated
mores, a place where a new culture and new politics could
thrive because there wasn't the old infrastructure in place
blocking everything. The American east coast in 1870
played the role of old Europe in the time of Sam Adams.

However, not all was progressive in Wyoming. By a
vote of 59-33, the 1869 Wyoming State Legislature voted
against gay marriage. The gays of Wyoming would have to
wait until June of 2015, when the U.S. Supreme Court told
all the states what was what.

30
"I'm Going to Cling to You, No Matter What Happens"

In 1848, Ulysses S. Grant took the plunge. He married Julia Wade Boggs Dent, the daughter of a plantation/slave owner who lived a little west of St. Louis.

How Ulysses popped the question is a nice story. One day, he was on a date with her when they had to cross a small bridge that was partially under water.

Julia was nervous. "I'm going to cling to you, no matter what happens," she said.

Ulysses replied, "How would you like to cling to me for the rest of your life?"

That was his proposal and it scored. The sly fox. That's a lot more romantic in my book than these pompous clods who propose to their girlfriend on the scoreboard at a football game.

Grant and Julia took the permanent cling on August 22, 1848.

31
Grant Meets King Edward - 1877

Almost as soon as he got out of office, Grant got out of town. With his wife Julia, and his son Jesse, the beleaguered ex-prez left the country for a grand tour of Europe. The Grants departed Philadelphia on May 17, 1877 on the cruise ship *Indiana*. Thousands were there to give the Grants one spectacular bon-voyage.

The first stop was Liverpool where he was welcomed as if he was Sir Paul McCartney. In London Grant checked into a five-star-general hotel. He was reading the paper and starting to crash when at about 9:00 p.m. he heard a knock on his door. He opened it up, and there before him stood none other than Edward the Fifth, the King of England!

Grant was scheduled to have a formal audience with the King the next day, but Edward decided to first make an informal social call. The two men cracked open a bottle and had a charming evening together, two giants in the calm eye of the hurricane. To be a fly on the wall for that one. The next day they were grandly introduced to each other at court and pretended to meet for the first time. I wish Americans running for President would do that before the debates. Set politics aside and break open a bottle together. Then they wouldn't want to break one over each other's head's the following day.

Grant went to Paris where the French treated him coldly, because they felt that the United States had sided with the Germans in the Franco-Prussian War of 1870-71.

Grant then went to Berlin where the Germans treated him warmly because they felt that the United States had sided with the Germans in the Franco-Prussian War of 1870-71.

32
Chicago Boston Panic – 1-2-3

A great fire destroyed the city of Chicago in October of 1871.

The fire began in Mrs. O'Leary's barn and was probably started by two guys; one of whom was nicknamed 'Peg-leg.' This hobo blamed it on Mrs. O'Leary's cow, claiming that "the dumb animal kicked over a lantern." History blames poor Mrs. O'Leary, when it was actually two male drunks that hung out in her barn who started it; probably with a discarded cigar or match.

The Chicago Fire burned for three days, October 8-10, 1871. More than three square miles in center city were destroyed. 300 people died, and more than 90,000 people were homeless for the winter.

The Chicago Fire was not a self-contained disaster. Chicago was an important commercial city and its partial destruction hurt the U.S. economy. On the other hand, the destroyed areas became a perfect site for the new 'skyscrapers' that were already being planned.

Just over a year later, on November 9, 1872, the downtown area of Boston, Massachusetts burned to the ground. 20 people died and monetary damage rivaled that of Chicago. Boston is, and was, a huge financial center of America. The two fires contributed to the downfall of a tottering economy by draining the big insurance companies of 273 million dollars.

This fiery tale of two cities helped to launch the Panic of 73.

33
President B. Gratz Brown

The Election of 1872 became a primary between two wings of the Republican Party with winner take the White House, and the Dems backing one of the wings of the Republicans.

The Democrats were tired of being beaten for President due to Civil War baggage, which was another reason they fell in with this strange-bedfellow arrangement. You couldn't wave the "bloody shirt" at a Northern Republican.

But the Democrats of '72 bet on the wrong horse in the form of Liberal Republican Horace Greely and they lost big in the Election of 1872.

Greely's candidacy in 1872 was a bad hand. Not only was Horace Greely slow and past his prime, but he died three weeks after the election on November 24, 1868. Even if he had won, he never would have taken office! Instead the next president would have been his VP, B. Gratz Brown.

34
<u>Who Needs Machine Guns –</u>
<u>June 26, 1876</u>

Custer might have put up a much tougher fight at The Battle of the Little Big Horn if he had listened to one of his lieutenants. Back at the base, a Lieutenant Saurette had advised Custer to take along some machine guns. Three Gatling guns were available. Even just a single one of these murder-machines might have turned the tide of battle. But confident Custer scoffed at the necessity of bringing machine guns to face "mere ignorant Indians."

Who's the ignoramus?

35
Johann Most

He was born in Bavaria in 1846 and died in Cincinnati in 1906. Johann Most was one of the most violent left wing bomb-throwing terrorists in all of American History. Mr. Most was an avowed anarchist who was arrested all over Europe before fleeing to America, where he was put in jail three times for advocating the violent overthrow of the United States government.

When McKinley was assassinated in 1901, Johann Most wrote a big article stating that it was no crime to kill any member of the ruling class. That got him in a bit of trouble, but he Most welcomed it. Johann was a Most irrational fellow.

In the famous Haymarket Bomb of 1886, one of the men who were executed for that crime had a letter in his possession showing how to build a stick of dynamite. It was written by Johann Most.

Johann published his own anarchist paper called "Freedom." Give me a break. Most also wrote a book about bomb-making called the *Science of Revolutionary Warfare*. His nickname was; I kid you not, "Dynamost."

When I first read about him I decided to add a little joke in my book that Johann Most was the grandfather of longtime Boston Celtics radio announcer Johnny Most. Then I found out he really was! Johann Most was the grandfather of Johnny Most! That explains why Johnny Most wanted to kill the referees every time they called a foul on the Celtics! Lunacy is a Johann Most family tradition.

36
A Heckler Makes a President - 1880

There was not a boatload of difference between the parties in any of the presidential contests of the years between Lincoln and McKinley. The choice was between the party of big business led by corrupt leaders (Reps) and the party of big business led by slightly less corrupt leaders (Dems). Neither party was a friend to the common laborer or the struggling farmer. Both parties believed in lassaizfaire economics at home, and a high tariff to keep the foreign competition out. Both rejected virtually all crazy reformist notions of the radical left, such as the eight-hour workday, the right to strike and a free education for all children.

The front-runner for 1880 was incumbent President Rutherford Hayes. Hayes, however, had pledged to serve only one-term and, unlike Theodore Roosevelt later on, he actually honored his commitment. The Republicans were mad at Hayes for firing NY Customs officers Roscoe Conkling and Chester Alan Arthur, and so they didn't want him anyway. Historian Candice Millard says that Hayes had become bitter over the fighting within the Republican Party and he told everyone he had therefore decided not to run for re-election in 1880, which makes it seem like they wanted him but he refused. But I get the impression that they didn't want him period; so that's quitting so they can't fire you. The accounts vary, but in any case, Hayes was out and the succession was up for grabs.

At the Republican Convention of 1880, the two favorites were Jim Blaine; the moderate reformer from Maine, and former President U.S. Grant. Also in the hunt were the acting Secretary of the Treasury James Sherman; 'the human icicle,' and Vermont Senator George Edmunds.

Ulysses Grant was out on an extensive overseas vacation after his grueling eight years of handing out undeserved jobs in Washington.

The two-term limitation was an unquestioned part of U.S. political tradition, but a band of Grant supporters devised slick reasons why it would be alright for him to run thrice. Grantites claimed that the "two term" rule applied only to two *consecutive* terms. Therefore Grant was eligible again. Congress heard about this and passed a resolution by a vote of 233-18 that any violation of the two-term tradition consecutive or otherwise would be "unwise, unpatriotic, and fraught with peril to our free institutions." FDR never read about it.

Ulysses Grant was the number one choice of the 'Stalwarts' and the choice also of that faction's intrepid leader, Roscoe Conkling of NY. The Stalwarts thought that the best jobs belonged to the best Republicans, not the best people. They were of the mind that the Republican Party was just fine as it was and did not need reforming. The passive Grant was perfect too, as far as they were concerned. The scandals within the Grant Administration didn't bother them enough to make a difference.

The Republicans met in Chicago for 400 speeches, making it truly the 'windy city.' The town that Billy Sunday couldn't shut down had been shut down in 1871 by the mother of all fires, and was still rebuilding devastated areas in 1880. The Convention was held at a new showpiece fireproof arena made of metal, not wood. The TD Bank Wigwam was ready when the Republican Convention of 1880 opened. This convention was more significant than it realized because it was electing the next two presidents.

There was so much opposition to Grant, even in his strongest states, that his supporters wisely tried to install a "unit-rule." The unit-rule meant that all delegates in a state had to vote for whatever candidate carried a majority in that state. Without the unit-rule Grant would lose a large number of delegates from the states he won and would probably have no chance against the other candidates like Blaine, Edmunds, and Sherman.

A little known politician from Ohio named James Garfield rose to oppose the unit-rule, as well as a couple of other proposals that happened to favor Grant's candidacy. In leading the fight that stopped the unit-rule, Garfield planted the seed that would lead to his presidency and early death. Garfield's unit-rule speech impressed everyone for his oratorical skills and he became a famous name overnight within the building.

Garfield made a speech the following evening nominating James Sherman for the presidency. In the middle of his speech he asked rhetorically, "And what is it we want?"

And, during the dramatic pause, a heckler yelled out, "We want James Garfield to be the next President of the United States!" The crowd laughed and Garfield blushed and plowed on with the speech. Garfield wanted to do his duty and honor to the man he was supposed to be supporting for president, Jimmy "Silver" Sherman, and he was ashamed that he had failed his friend.

The heckle was the lead story on that speech, stealing a chance for Sherman to get some juice. On the first ballot, one heckler-inspired Republican delegate voted for James A. Garfield for president.

The Chicago Convention was the most boisterous American political convention to date. The cheering and hissing and demonstrations for men and resolutions were such that one newspaper said they acted "like so many Bedlamites." Bedlam at the time was an actual place in London filled with lunatics.

When the Republican Convention of 1880 closed, the term 'bedlam' joined the dictionary with a small 'b' to mean a place in a condition of lunacy. Today the old Bedlam building is the home of the Imperial War Museum, and it's a close call which one stands for more insanity.

Grant led on the first ballot, with Blaine a close second and Sherman third. All three had strong support, but none enough to win. Among many scattered lesser candidates, there was that one lingering vote for Garfield.

Thirty-three more ballots followed with no change. On the 34th ballot 17 votes showed up for James Garfield. The Ohioan won 50 votes on the 35th ballot and the momentum suddenly went overwhelmingly Jimmy's way.

Garfield protested at every step along the way, and sincerely. He did not come to Chicago to become President of the United States. He only wanted to help out with the Convention, see a Cubs game, and maybe bribe a cop. He especially did not want it to appear that he had betrayed James Sherman, the man he nominated and was pledged to support. But it was too late. Blaine and Sherman both disliked Grant (some historians say "hated"). They would, however, much rather lose the nomination to Garfield than to continue in a hopeless deadlock against strongman Ulysses. James and James threw their support to James Garfield and on the 36th ballot it was all over.

The whole thing served Sherman right. Senator Sherman knew that Garfield had potential as a rival candidate and thought he could neutralize him by asking him to give the nominating speech. Garfield had turned the tables on Sherman, but not deliberately.

Garfield was completely stunned when the hall nominated him by acclaim. The place went bananas. He had shown up as a passive, polite delegate and all of a sudden he was the nominee. Mobs were crowding him in celebration as he made his way with some effort out the back door to find his driver to take him back to the Hotel Quigley. The poor driver had no idea that his polite client had just won the nomination for president. The teamster didn't know what was going on when hundreds surrounded his horse and buggy as Garfield climbed into it. The adoring mob decided that they would unhook the horses and take their champion back to the hotel on their shoulders, a triumphant jolly trip through the city of big shoulders. But the driver didn't know that. He just felt threatened and he proceeded to use his whip to lash the crowd away from the vehicle. Several were stung hard and the driver took off and got Garfield back to the hotel.

So the next time you see a bunch of dorks over-doing it at a big political convention on TV, and say to yourself, "These clowns should be horsewhipped," you can take some satisfaction in knowing that it did happen once.

37
<u>Lights! – September 4, 1882</u>

On September 4, 1882, a new era in America began at dusk. Amidst great ceremony, Tommy Edison flipped a switch and 26 buildings in New York City turned night into day. Electricity had arrived in America.

Edison had invented it in 1878 and tried it out successfully in Menlo Park, New Jersey on New Year's Eve 1880. TE now made it the real deal by lighting up the New York Stock Exchange, The New York Times, City Hall, Ratner's Diner, Catch a Rising Star, and 20 other structures all in one dramatic moment. Oh, to have been there to see that!

J.P. Morgan had bankrolled Edison's work. Edison soon founded GE and Moneybags Morgan bought into that too.

38
Sitting Bull and the Golden Spike – September 8, 1883

Sitting Bull and the Northern Pacific Railroad provide the backdrop for this next story, which took place on September 8, 1883.

Sitting Bull, the Chief of the Hunkpapa Sioux Indians, had come back from Canada with his tribe in 1881. The whites put him in jail in a treacherous breach of faith regarding the terms for his return. SB was supposed to get an amnesty and a promise of government help for his suffering people.

The great Northern Pacific Railroad was scheduled to connect at last on September 8, 1883. It would be a couple of years before all was finished and a train could run from St Paul to Portland, but the two lines had at least linked up in the summer of 83. A "Golden Spike" ceremony was scheduled for Bismarck, South Dakota on the same day the actual spike was driven at Gold Creek, Montana.

The white government thought it would be fitting if a famous Indian participated in the celebration ceremony. They asked Sitting Bull to come to Bismarck on the fateful day and complete the picture. Bull agreed and even tried to memorize a short speech in English, or so he told them. There would be a bilingual white man there in case his speech was indecipherable and a translation was needed.

When the time came for SB to make the speech in SD, he dropped any attempt to speak English. Sitting Bull spoke in his Sioux language. The translator was ready. So was Sitting. The head Hunkpapa gave a nine-minute speech and didn't stop to let the translator in. So the translator made notes and waited for Bull to finish.

With each couple of sentences Sitting Bull would pause and briefly scan the audience with a stern countenance. The crowd took the cue and applauded each time. What the crowd didn't know was that Sitting Bull had started his speech this way:

"You white people are all liars and thieves and

cowards. You have mistreated my people and then lied about it. You make promises you know you will break. You all make me sick..."

And it got worse from there. When Bull finished and sat down with a wry smile, the white translator cleared his throat and ad-libbed a harmless positive speech that Sitting Bull was honored to be there and thankful that the Great Father had brought so much progress to the wilderness.

39
Jeanne De Puysieux – The Statue of Liberty - 1886

It took 10 years for the French to build it, ship it, and help set it up. The Statue of Liberty, 305 feet tall, was dedicated in NYC at long last on October 28, 1886. Thousands of dignitaries were on hand, including President Cleveland and Betty White.

Liberty was a centennial gift from the French, perhaps reminding the United States in a subtle way that France had been the key to the success of the Revolution of 1776.

Even now it is an impressive and mammoth work. Imagine how awesome it must have seemed in 1886. I've been up it once. Most New Yorkers have never been there and swear that they have been meaning to go there for some time.

The Statue had been ready for almost two years, but the pedestal had to be completed before it could stand up and open for business. Libby served a practical purpose for many years as a harbor lighthouse until 1902.

Most Americans were not terribly excited about the big girl at first. But the immigrants made her a great lady. They were moved when they passed it on the way to Ellis Island. They loved it and all it stood for, and their emotions fueled the rise in its charismatic reputation.

The sculptor was Fred Bartholdi. He used two different women as models. The first was his mother, Madame Bartholdi. But Mrs. B. wasn't quite statuesque enough. Fred replaced his mother with his mistress, Jeanne-Emilie de Puysieux. Fred met Jean while on a trip to Washington D.C., long before the statue was born. They were living in sin in France while he worked on the statue.

As the date for the dedication approached, the story got around in America that the Statue of Liberty was modeled after a woman who let men take liberties. "That's how she got her name," went the popular joke.

Bartholdi felt the pressure. And so, in the best interest of both countries, and hopefully because he really loved her, Fred Bartholdi made an honest woman out of the Statue of Liberty. He married Jeanne de Puysieux. He put a ring on that left hand holding the torch.

40
The Samoan Crisis of 1885-1889

The USA almost went to war with Germany in the 1800's over Samoa. The Samoan Crisis began under Cleveland's first term and was not resolved until well into the presidency of Benjamin Harrison. The Navigator Islands in the southwest Pacific, better known as the Samoans, were of strategic naval importance to the USA and Great Britain, and of commercial importance to Germany. All three nations had their eyes on the Samoan prize in Cleveland's time.

The Samoans still ruled their own land at the beginning of the 1800's. The Europeans had "discovered" them, but had left them alone until they could "discover" a way to exploit and dominate them. The Germans started that colonial ball rolling in the mid 1800's. German traders wanted Otto Bismarck to annex Samoa, but Otto wouldn't go that far. So the German traders were then willing to settle for any foreign control as long as they could carry on their trade.

New Zealand worried about a German-controlled Samoa which would threaten the lines of communication and trade between Australia, New Zealand and the Americas.

The United States shared some of this concern and wanted at least one naval base in the Samoans for its big modern navy, which was just then being built. Britain was backing Australia and New Zealand, of course, and wanted a Samoan base for the Royal Navy there as well.

Germany continued to build up its influence in Samoa, buying land from naive natives, who didn't realize what they were selling, nor who they were selling out to.

The United States, Great Britain and Germany were all converging on Samoa.

Malietoa Laupepa was the King of Samoa. In 1884 Germany forced him to sign a treaty making the islands a German protectorate in return for a few small favors. King Laupepa was paying for mob protection. This was a form of surrender with the word "protectorate" used to assuage the conscience of Germany and to make a good cover story for world media consumption.

King Laupepa did not take it lying down. He and 48 tribal leaders made a formal protest about German aggression to Great Britain, asking for British intervention. You know your back is to the wall when you ask for the British to take over your country as a favor to you.

Germany wised up and tried to disguise the protectorate business under a new mask. The Germans installed a puppet Samoan King named Tamassee to rule the islands. This set off a fighting civil war between the loyal rebels (oxymoronic, I know) and the troops of the puppet king Tamassee.

German and Britain began to talk of a three-way sharing of colonialist power in Samoa. The USA did not care for this idea. Secretary of State Bayard filed a formal protest with the German government in Berlin. America opposed German actions in Samoa and wanted no part of the triple vulture plan.

Unfortunately for Cleveland, this was the only idea Germany was offering. Beyond that it was 'now, are you going to do something about it?' The deciding vote was Britain and, sadly, they backed the German idea of triple vulture. The British reminded the Americans that everyone was going to make a lot of money, and everyone gets a naval base too.

Cleveland and Bayard countered with a question. What would happen if a dispute broke out between any in the group while their Pacific fleets sat with guns drawn right beside each other? That question concerned a few diplomats in all three countries.

Bayard requested a three-power conference in D.C. to discuss the fate of the helpless mouse at their mercy in the South Central Pacific.

The conference took place in 1888. The Washington hosts were disappointed to see that they faced Germany and the UK standing united against the United States.

Great Britain had made a logrolling deal with Germany. The British would support Germany in Samoa and in its claims to other Pacific islands if Germany would remain passive about British foreign policy goals in the Middle

East, especially Egypt.

The Washington Conference of 1888 came to nothing. Britain was not negotiating over Samoa at face value. Naturally, no one from Samoa was invited to attend the Conference.

Germany soon raised its national flag over the capital of Apia. A Mr. Brandeis was named as the Kaiser of Samoa. There was no longer even a pretense of native rule. Britain was not going to help Cleveland because of that old-style deal it had made regarding Egypt. German police officials in Samoa began to intimidate Americans living and trading there. Germany wanted the USA to get out. German Samoa passed laws discriminating against Americans, while ignoring the protests of Secretary of State Tommy Bayard.

In January of 1889, Cleveland presented the Samoan dispute to Congress for its consideration, an act which could lead to a Congressional proposal for war that Cleveland would sign, rather than the reverse, which he could have tried. This bold act by a lame duck President got the Germans' attention. Bismarck requested a resumption of the ole' three-power negotiations; this time in Berlin.

Germany now backed off a bit. It had its hands full in Samoa with a new round of civil war going on between the Germans and their quislings, and a rebel named Mataafa, who took over the fight from Malietoa. America wouldn't agree to a conference until Germany made peace with the rebels. They did, and the Berlin Conference began.

The United States already had a preponderant influence over the eastern Samoan Island of Tutuila with its fine harbor of Pago Pago. But Germany was threatening to annex its western islands outright.

President Harrison took over for Cleveland. He was no more amenable to the triple vulture idea than Cleveland had been. This was all the Germans offered the U.S. at Berlin. The same old deal...or no deal. Kaiser's way or the highway.

The United States sent warships to hang out in Apia harbor. The British had a couple of modern naval ships there too. It was a stand-off between the American and German warships with the British as an interested third presence trying to remain neutral. The U.S. naval ships were made of wood. Only one ship in the three fleets was of modern steel construction.

Tension was near the breaking point when a storm blew out the fire. On the night of March 15-16, 1889 a breathtaking typhoon struck Apia harbor. The storm destroyed or beached all the warships in the Samoas except one; the British steeler *Calliope*. More than 53 U.S. sailors died in the storm and more than 90 Germans went kaput. It was weather changing history and politics. With no naval pawns to do their bidding, the three antagonists had little alternative but to negotiate a peaceful settlement of the Samoan stand-off. Mother Nature had taken their guns away. Benjamin Harrison and the Congress were suddenly willing to accept the triple overseer arrangement of the three big powers in Samoa.

The Samoan Kamikaze was a divine message to the USA to modernize its Navy. First a crisis with Chile during which Chile had the stronger navy, now this. Enough. Congress hove to and appropriated the construction of a slew of big steel battleships.

The Samoan Crisis of 1889 was over, but America had won itself an enemy. Germany was offended by the whole affair. The Kaiser unfriended President Harrison on Facebook. The crisis in Samoa helped to draw the battle lines for the USA later on in WWI.

The USA obtained one of the Samoan Islands in the final treaty, while England agreed to drop out of the Samoan sweepstakes in exchange for concessions by both countries in other spheres of interest.

Today the eastern Samoan Islands are still part of the United States of America. American Samoa has given America many excellent NFL players.

Robert Louis Stevenson of *Treasure Island* fame wrote a fine history of the Samoan Islands controversy of 1885-89. Not that I read it, but anything written by Robert Louis Stevenson has to be fine.

41

The Bradley-Martin Ball - $387,334.35 – February 10, 1897

On February 10, 1897 the richest elitists in New York City threw the best party of all-time and, in the process, threw themselves a curve-ball. The Bradley-Martin Ball at the Waldorf-Astoria caused a vicious backlash against the rich. The party was a flop in that sense, but it was some party, nevertheless.

Beatrice Langley had some money and then married a very rich guy named Bradley Martin. She not only adopted his last name, she adopted his first name too. Beatrice legally took the married name of Mrs. Bradley-Martin. That's a far cry from today's women who so often keep their own last name in the middle. But Beatrice knew how to move in social circles and did it better as a Bradley-Martin.

Mrs. Bradley-Martin decided to throw the best party in the history of the world. "Go for the gusto or don't go at all," was her motto. The prince is having a ball, a costume ball at the Waldorf. The party was deliberately arranged on short notice so that the rich revelers would have to "buy American."

Yes, there was supposedly a noble motive at work. Mrs. Bradley-Martin felt bad that the U.S. clothing industry was at a near standstill, and felt that the upper class was partly responsible because they bought all their clothes from Paris, London, and Rome. So let's throw a huge party for the filthy rich on short notice, make it a costume ball, and force the rich to help the New York made-in-the-USA fashion industry. Hopefully there might be some trickle down help for the whole country.

Well, at least that was their story after the whole thing caused such a furor.

The party was a big hit for those who were lucky enough to be there. Millionaires arrived in the most fantastic, expensive costumes. The spread was fit for a king. The drinks, the hors d'oeuvres, the music, the butlers, and the main course were all the most expensive in the world. There was a diamond-throwing contest at 6.

The public reaction was pronounced, and all bad. The party cost the Bradley-Martins a total of $387,334.35, and this in an era when a dollar was a day's wage. Newspapers printed the figure of $387.334.35 in giant headlines, and condemned the whole affair with passion. Beatrice Bradley-Martin became the Marie Antoinette of the American class struggle. Preachers in the pulpit excoriated the rich revelers to shreds, reminding listeners of the day that Christ lost his cool with the money-changers. Few if anyone bought the Bradley-Martin story that it was all to help the garment industry. Few even heard about that angle, let alone bought it. The guilty rich couldn't even get their cover story out there very much.

Punishment was in order. The New York City tax collectors singled out the Bradley-Martins and, in an act of selective punitive socialism, raised their tax rates to triple what all their other rich neighbors were paying.

There was no justification for taxing the Bradley-Martins in punishment, and there is plenty of justification for spending as much as one damn well pleases on a private party. That's the way I see it. That's the way the Martins saw it too, and they moved to England in a huff. A lot of history books make it seem as if the public anger intimidated them to move; like they were almost afraid of being harmed. It was more of a defiant gesture, and they already had a fourth home in England, so it wasn't like they arrived in Liverpool wiping the sweat from their brow and saying, "whew, that was a close call." But some of the accounts make it seem like that.

I wish I could have gone to that party.

42
Capture of Aguinaldo – March 23,1901

When America won the war with Spain it inherited the Philippines. But the people of the Philippines wanted independence. They did not want to be ruled by United States any more than they had wanted Spain to rule over them.

The Philippines resisted American occupation and so began the Philippine Insurrection of 1901-03, a full scale war between American and Filipino soldiers.

The Philippine rebels fought hard and the war was as savage as wars get. There were sadistic atrocities on both sides. The rebel leader was Emilio Aguinaldo, and the Americans wanted badly to capture him. The Americans had all the firepower in the War of the Philippine Insurrection, but they still had to checkmate the king. As long as iconic Emilio was on the loose in the Pacific jungles, the Insurrection was never over. Aguinaldo was the moral, political and military leader of the Philippine Insurrection.

The Americans won a succession of battles, but that wasn't enough. And no one knew where Aguinaldo was. He was a rebel on the run with his band of political assassins aspiring to be a real army. He had a small fighting force with him but his odds were getting worse by the day.

The beginning of the end came when the Americans captured one of Aguinaldo's messengers and he "talked." The traitor's name was Cecilio Segismundo. Cecil later claimed that he only gave his leader away because the Americans tortured him. The Yanks insisted that Cecil had copped out without being physically abused in any way.

For whatever reason, Siggy sang. He tipped the USA off to the whereabouts of the little brown king. Aguinaldo was at Palinan, Luzon.

The U.S. Army devised a plan to capture Aguinaldo. It involved intrigue and adventure, it employed virtually no military force, and it worked.

The plan was the brainstorm of Fred Funston, a brigadier general. Funston knew that Aguinaldo was hoping to get reinforcements at his headquarters in the town of Palinan in northeastern Luzon. Funston's plan was dangerous, audacious and deceptive.

The Americans would send Aguinaldo a fake reinforcement battalion of insurrectos right to his front door at Palinan. And they had American prisoners with them. Or did they?

Cecil the traitor would lead the Trojan Horse battalion, with Mop Lazaro, another dependable Filipino "loyalist" at his side. The Yanks hired as fake Filipino reinforcements the Macabebes, tribesmen who had served Spain when Spain ruled in return for a little autonomy. Working for Uncle Sam was no problem on their conscience. The Macabebes were the Cossacks of the Philippine Insurrection and had a reputation for fierce fighting. It was a dangerous mission, and they didn't mind.

General Arthur MacArthur approved the plan. Fake Rebel reinforcement units set sail for Casiguran Bay in Luzon where they landed on Valentine's Day 1901.

The men pretended to be dragging American prisoners for delivery to Aguinaldo. The squad marched overland for five weeks. The rebel populace cheered them as heroes as they passed through. The Macabebes even hit their prisoners now and then with bamboo sticks to make it look good. And they smacked them hard, too, just to be safe.

Word travelled ahead of the mission. Emilio broke into a big grin when he heard that the reinforcements were on the way. He was especially pleased to hear that the relief party had five American prisoners, including an officer. Emilio sent some of his best fighters out to meet the party in advance and take charge of the American prisoners. Funston and Lazaro had to think fast when Aguinaldo's scouts approached.

The fake insurrectos quickly hid the fake prisoners in the jungle and claimed that the POW's had never left the beach, and were "in a cage back at Casiguran Bay." Augie's scouts bought that line. The rebel saps continued on towards Casiguran Bay to pick up the prisoners who weren't there, while the double-dealing relief battalion marched on towards Aguinaldo with the fake prisoners.

Cecil, Laz and company entered Aguinaldo's village with the prisoners in chains. They showed off their glum prisoners. The rebel leader Aguinaldo was on the second floor of his HQ looking out the window as he saw the reinforcement brigade enter the square below. The fake rebels lowered their guns and began to make small talk with the real rebels in the square while a small party under Cecil and Laz went upstairs to greet and chat with Emilio. Aguinaldo thanked them profusely. They all hugged him and said that no one would rest until the dirty Yankees were booted out of the Philippines. Emilio smiled warmly and made a joke. They all began to joke around about little things. Aguinaldo was laughing as Lazaro went to the window and watched below as his Macabebe double agents wandered about while slyly positioning themselves behind the real insurrectos. Laz gave a signal from the window. The Macabebes made their move, attacking some, shooting some, throwing some to the ground, and getting others to raise their hands in surrender.

Aguinaldo heard the shooting in the middle of his chatting and ran angrily to the window to tell his men to stop shooting rounds off like it is was a drunken party. He didn't realize what was going on until Cecil and Lazaro threw him to the ground and put him in a headlock and told him to "say uncle!"

And he did. "All right I give! We give! Uncle Sam! Uncle Sam!"

A few loyal rebels tried to break into the room to save Aguinaldo, but Placido and Cecilio shot them down.

Just moments after Aguinaldo realized that he had been tricked, Frederick Funston entered the room and said, "You are being taken prisoner in the name of the United States. President McKinley sends his greetings." Since Placido and Laz were sitting on his back at the time, Emilio decided not to resist.

Aguinaldo surrendered formally. Within an hour he seemed at ease with the whole situation. At least now he might live for a while. Being the #1 bandito was dangerous work.

The Yanks and Macs brought him in chains to Manila on March 28. On April 28 Aguinaldo took an oath of loyalty to the United States and asked his followers to do the same. No more chains.

Even with their fearless leader captured, the insurrectos still had plenty to fight for, but they were a ship without a rudder. The Insurrection did not end just like that, right then and there, but the capture of Aguinaldo was the watershed event in the conflict. There was much bloody sporadic fighting to go yet, but from then on the Americans had the momentum.

Aguinaldo later emigrated to the USA, lived to be almost 80 years old, and died in Hammondsport, NY in 1953 as the proud owner of two wine vineyards.

43
Trolley Hits Bull Moose – Pittsfield, MA – September 3, 1902

In August 1902, President Theodore Roosevelt began a tour of New England. It was all productive and smooth until the last leg when Teddy almost lost his leg in a trolley crash. The President almost died from this leg injury. And it happened in Pittsfield, MA.

Teddy spent the night of September 2, 1902 at the home of Massachusetts Governor Crane in Dalton (where U.S. greenback paper is exclusively manufactured today). Dalton is at the far western end of Massachusetts.

TR had one last New England travel-round planned, a ride from Dalton to Lenox via the city of Pittsfield. His entire trip was a matter of high publicity and everywhere he went the crowds gathered to stare at the Bull Moose, hear his speeches, or shake his vigorous hand.

Roosevelt's party travelled by way of a top-quality horse-drawn wagon (called a "barouche"). There were five men in the wagon as it approached Pittsfield. They were President Roosevelt, Governor Crane, Roosevelt's personal secretary George Cortleyou, the driver Stuart Lane, and Billy Craig; a member of the secret service.

Several trolley lines crisscrossed Pittsfield. These trolleys were big steam powered trains, not to be taken lightly by pedestrians, or horse drawn carriages. On that day, all trolleys were packed to the hilt with people who were hoping to be on the right train at the right time when the charismatic Prez passed through Pittsfield. The trolley operators were running at top speeds looking for the President's carriage so that their lucky riders would catch a glimpse of the big star. The trolleys were thus accidentally on purpose overcrowded and going too fast.

TR's carriage was crossing one of the tracks when it was broadsided at about 35 miles per hour by one of the rubbernecking trolleys. TR's driver was seriously injured. Teddy Roosevelt, Cortleyou and Governor Crane flew through the air and crashed to the street. All three were covered with cuts and bruises. They laid on the street moaning. In a brief moment of shock no pedestrian even moved to help them. There was more focus on the poor secret serviceman Billy Craig. He was the one man who had not been thrown from the vehicle. Billy was crushed between the two machines, one of wood the other of steel. Billy Craig was dead, the first secret serviceman killed in the line of duty in American history.

Of the three celebrities, Roosevelt was the most seriously hurt, but he put up such a tough-man front that he managed to deny it, even to himself. He knew that his leg was hurting bad, but he was sure it wasn't broken so that was enough. TR went on with the trip to Lenox claiming that, "the Spanish couldn't hurt me and neither can the Trolleys of Pittsfield."

TR that night was grinning and shaking hands in Lenox. No one cared that he was limping. They wanted to touch greatness. They didn't know it, but they were shaking hands with stupidity.

What Roosevelt didn't realize was that the pain in his leg was blood poisoning. Roosevelt kept traveling the nation giving speeches and visiting politicians. On September 24, at Indianapolis, President Roosevelt was dizzy with pain. He finally gave in and rushed back to Washington for repairs. D.C. doctors had to operate to the bone and clean out an obvious abscess. Roosevelt could have lost a leg and could have died. America could have lost the President to a premature death, because he was acting like a fool.

If TR had died in Pittsfield the USA would have lost two sitting presidents to the grave within a span of a single year.

44
<u>Perdicaris Fever – Algiers 1904</u>

In late May 1904 President Roosevelt received word of an insult to the flag from Islamic terrorists in the Middle East. It seemed that a well-to-do American citizen by the name of Ion Perdicaris was sipping expensive tea on his patio in Algiers when Berber rebels attacked. The Berber Rebs were trying to overthrow the government of Morocco. The intruders roughed up the aristocratic house guests and made off with two hostages, Ion Perdicaris and his nephew Clarence.

The leader of the attack was a Berber named Raisuli. He was ruthless. They called him "Berber the Barber." He didn't have anything against Perdicaris personally, nor against the USA. But he wanted to force the rulers of Morocco into granting his political demands by holding a prominent Westerner hostage. The Moroccan government would need to avoid trouble with the western powers and would prefer political concessions to Moroccan rebels over diplomatic entanglements with disgruntled superpowers.

The plan in the end essentially worked, as the American was released when the Moroccan government agreed to Raisuli's demands. But a lot happened in between the beginning and end of the story.

Teddy Roosevelt didn't miss his chance to play tough-guy. He issued angry statements to both the Raisuli rebels and to the Moroccan government.

In mid-June Washington learned that Ion Perdicaris was only pretending to be an American citizen. He had lived for some time in New Jersey, but when Raisuli kidnapped him, Perdicaris was a Greek citizen, in Morocco on a Greek passport.

Roosevelt and Secretary of State John Hay decided that this was essentially irrelevant since Raisuli *thought* that Ion was an American when he kidnapped him. Hay was sometimes almost as rough riding as his boss. Hay and TR agreed that what mattered was that the entire world thought that Perdicaris was an American citizen, and the story had already swept the globe that way. Jack Hay and TR decided not to let the public know that the man named Perdicaris was a Greek. American honor was still on the line; even if American lives were in fact not. Perception is fact.

The President dispatched seven battleships to Morocco to make it clear that the USA wasn't going to take any guff from these scruffs. At one point ten U.S. Marines went ashore to guard the American Embassy, but this was reported in some dispatches as "an assault by U.S. troops."

The Americans were sending mixed signals. Along with the warships, went the ransom payment. It was the cash; not the threats, that secured Perdicaris' release along with that of his bewildered nephew.

What was more embarrassing to the Roosevelt posture was that Perdicaris had grown fond of his captors and was releasing statements to the press defending his kidnappers! It was "Stockholm syndrome" about 65 years before that term was coined. Perdicaris described Raisuli as "a swell guy." TR threw the newspaper at the wall when he read that one.

There was a movie based on the kidnapping of Perdicaris called *The Wind and the Lion*. Sean Connery plays Raisuli. When a movie is "based on" a true story, it's the same as saying its loaded with lies in the name of drama. In *Wind and Lion*, Raisuli kidnaps a beautiful rich American woman who hates him at first and then they fall in love. Oh, brother. U.S. Marines land in brigade force on the beaches in Morocco and engage in full-scale battle with both German and Moroccan troops. People are dying all over the screen. Drama drowns out the truth; what else is new?

The Perdicaris story was part of the campaign for President in 1904. In June the Republican National Convention met in Chicago. The Perdicaris situation was as yet unresolved and was continuous headline news. Roosevelt issued a statement to be read to the convention on the 22nd of June:

"We want either Perdicaris alive or Raisuli dead!"

45
The Wright Brothers Give Up –
1905-1908

On December 17, 1903 the Wright Brothers, Orville and Wilbur, made the first successful airplane flight at Kitty Hawk, North Carolina. It was an incredible achievement. Literally. America's newspaper editors simply didn't believe the reports or scoffed at the story as a prankster's hoax and printed a cynical denial. The only newspaper that printed the story at face value was in Dayton, Ohio, a short perfunctory blurb on page nine - and that was printed only because both Wrights were from Dayton Ohio. Search the microfilms for headlines about the first flight and you'll get nothing.

The Wrights soared some more in 1904. People in the immediate area were excited and thrilled, but again, by the time the story reached big city newspapers, the crusty old editors dismissed them as false tales. They did not believe that two guys from a bike shop had invented a heavier than air craft made of wood and metal that could fly two guys in circles at will for two hours and land them safely with the plane undamaged.

The Wrights made more planes and flew them in many places. They dazzled the crowds. But the media wasn't inter-connected and vast like it is now. No one could verify the flight to the satisfaction of these newspaper people, and no one on behalf of the Wrights crusaded to get their story out and verified either. The Wrights couldn't get their invention taken seriously by anyone except immediate observers. The rubes cheered while the sophisticates ignored.

And so...the Wright Brothers gave up. Between October 1905 and May 1908, the Wright Brothers didn't even bother to fly anymore!

The Wrights tried to get the U. S. government interested in buying the new invention, but D.C. wasn't interested.

But the French were not so naïve. When the Wrights

shipped a plane over to France and then went over there with it for a test drive, the entire French nation went haywire. The headlines all over the country screamed the glorious news of the magnificent Wrights and their flying machine.

All of a sudden the U.S. government became quite interested in the airplane. Copycats began building their own version. In late 08 the U.S. Army bought its first plane from a competitor of the Wrights for $6,300. The Wrights soon came under U.S. contract as well.

To me, this story of no one believing the Wright Brothers is nothing short of amazing.

46
San Francisco Earthquake – April 18, 1906

At 5:18 in the morning of April 18, 1906, an earthquake of 7.7 on the Richter Scale rocked the San Francisco Bay area. For 42 seconds Frisco shook as if some giant monster was a gold prospector shaking his pan with a city in it. Thousands of buildings came down like houses of cards. Approximately 3,243 people died. Fires broke out and could not be contained for three days.

80% of the city of San Francisco was gone. The quake killed people in San Jose and Santa Rosa as well.

Dynamite teams tried to stop the fire through tactical explosions, but they actually caused it to spread further. Mayor Nagan blamed FEMA for starting the fire.

There had been a series of medium size (in other words, kind of scary) earthquakes in and around San Francisco in the decade leading up the big one. The old timers had never seen such a high number of medium bad quakes, but everyone figured that life goes on and what can you do? Whatever happens, happens. It happened.

For the next 40 years or so, every hustler in America claimed to be born in San Francisco. Since all government records burned in the great fire, any grifter could claim to be anybody as long as they were supposedly born in San Francisco.

47

Brain Storm – The Girl on the Red Velvet Swing - 1906

In June 1906, the trial of a well-to-do patron of the arts named Harry Kendall Thaw gave American slang a new term: 'brain-storm.'

Thaw committed a murder that gripped America in gossip for months and even years. Historian Mark Sullivan calls the trial of Harry Thaw the "most sensational in the history of the country." Harry killed Harry. The victim was named Harry Stanford White.

The case was spectacular for three main reasons. The murdered man was a rich celebrity. The crime took place in a posh downtown NYC theatre in the middle of a sold-out performance by big-name actors. The triggerman was declared not guilty by reason of insanity, which triggered a major national debate over the use of that defense in a court of law.

The high-priced lawyer defending Thaw told the jury to show mercy because his client was under the influence of a "brain-storm" when he killed. "Brain-storm" made for good headlines and the term caught on with the public. The term has evolved into a more positive meaning as a creative inspirational storm, a winning idea that saves the day, but back in 1906 'brain-storm' meant a storm of dark thunder clouds inside an off-balanced murderous brain.

In the current era one can buy a ticket to see the New York Knicks get "murdered" at Madison Square Garden by a visiting team. But if you were attending a show at the original Madison Square Garden on June 25, 1906 you might have witnessed the murder of a famous millionaire architect named Harry Stanford White. White had designed the building. He had built his own coffin.

Madison Square Garden today is a dilution of the concept. In 1906 it was a building of several entertainment venues, all of them blended into a tapestry of real gardens. Newspaper paintings of the murder sequence show fancy plants and water décor all about.

The killer and the victim were both celebrities. We do love to read how the mighty fall. In the Thaw-White slaying of June 06 we have one of the richest men in the USA shooting one of the other richest men. It was as if Donald trump saw Bill Gates at a crap table in Atlantic City and shot him dead, ruining a lovely felt green table with blood.

And what was it all about?

Harry K. Thaw was in love with a woman named Alice Nesbitt. But famous architect Harry S. White had also gone out with her years earlier, when she was very young and looked like a young Joan Collins. Miss Nesbitt wasn't married at the time that Mr. White allegedly "seduced her." In 1906 this was rather a big deal. There was a big age difference between Harry S. White and Young Alice Nesbitt. It wasn't quite as big as the age difference in a contemporary movie between an aged male Hollywood big-draw and his girl-friend, an unknown actress, but it was big.

Harry White was a dedicated swinging bachelor. Allegedly, the stupid flirt joke, "Come upstairs and see my etchings," originated with Harry White and his studio containing the infamous red velvet swing. HW had a red swing for his ladies to pose on while he drew them.

So Harry Kendall Thaw married Alice Nesbitt and didn't like the stories he discovered about the good times she had way back when with Harry Stanford White.

Thaw went to Madison Square Garden to see a vaudeville comedy show *The American Mistress* (ironically) on the night of June 25, 1906. Once an hour on the hour, Thaw walked past White's table and gave him a dirty look. Harry was well aware that Harry hated him.

In 1865 John Wilkes Booth waited for the big punch line in *"My American Cousin"* before he pulled the trigger. Thaw must have been a student of the Lincoln assassination. He timed it.

Thaw waited for a big laugh to strike on. The baggy-pants clown said "I have a mistress up in Maine. I go up to Bangor every week!" Thaw waited for the big laugh, then appeared suddenly before White, drew a pistol and shot White three times in the face. That's not even easy to do.

The laughing audience heard the shots, but thought the shooting was actually part of the show! But when two people close by saw White's face they screamed like a woman in a Vincent Price film, and the audience bolted for the exits. Thaw surrendered matter-of-factly to the nearest cop.

H.K. Thaw had the money for expensive talented lawyers. He got his dream team to spin an angle. Harry Stanford White had defiled the womanhood of this Harry Kendall Thaw's wife. So what if it happened years before they were married, he had still done it. "Mr. Thaw had a brainstorm!" yelled the lawyer. "In avenging the ruination of his wife's good name, he was protecting his home and was defending the womanhood of the nation!"

The trial lasted some time. The nation followed it religiously. Rich people killing rich people is relatively rare. There's not a lot to be mad about when you're rich. Maybe that's why the jury declared insanity. What sane rich person wants to kill anyone? Having murder in your heart is the specialty of the poor. Trust me on that one.

Thaw was acquitted by reason of insanity. He spent less than eight years in a looney bin and then went on to lead a long life. He still had dough. Alice Nesbitt got a divorce and went into vaudeville as a novelty act, The Girl on the Red Velvet Swing.

They made a movie called the *The Girl in the Red Velvet Swing* starring Ray Milland as Harry Kendall Thaw and Pia Zadora as Alice Nesbitt. This Paramount film twists the story around so much I can only borderline recommend it.

48
Russian Lady Takes Out a Cigarette - 1910

Back in Taft's time it was a controversial subject. Was it all right for women to smoke?

The older folks said, "No! Well I never! The very idea!" The younger folks said, "Spark it up, Dianne. And blow the smoke in grandfather's angry face." The new generation of young people was revising the morals of America. Female smoking was as good a place to make a stand as any other.

One day in 1910 Alice Roosevelt came to visit the White House at a William Taft ball. Alice started to light up a cigarette and a man named Archie Butt (I kid you not) butted in and told her to put that butt out. Alice, always a defiant one anyway, shrugged her shoulders, and brought her cigarette up to the White House roof where she smoked to her rebel heart's content while watching the Pennsylvania Ave traffic stroll by.

Sixty-seven years later President Carter's aide Hamilton Jordan, and pop music star Willie Nelson continued the Alice Roosevelt tradition and also smoked rebelliously on the White House roof. But it was a different brand of tobacco than the one Alice was smoking. In fact Willie Nelson later claimed that after he was finished he actually spoke with Alice Roosevelt.

On another occasion a Russian lady of some renown visited the Taft White House, and when she took out a cigarette, the others nearby gasped in horror. Taft, the big gentleman that he was, shocked everyone even more when he lit it up for her. The President's aides pressed the press to not report it, and they didn't.

49
__Archie Butt__

One of the most famous men of his era, but little remembered today, was the above mentioned Archie Butt. Butt was a close advisor and friend to Presidents Theodore Roosevelt and William Howard Taft.

A.B. was a lifelong military man, having served in both the Spanish-American War and the Philippine Insurrection. He was not officially a TR or Taft cabinet member, but Arch had more personal access to the President than any three official cabinet members combined. Military advisor, golfing buddy, valet, personal advisor; not a yes man, but always supportive, Archie Butt was an important presence in two Administrations. He's in a lot of pictures from both eras. Archie's the guy in full military dress standing behind or somewhere near the President.

When Taft and Roosevelt had their tragic quarrel, Archie was caught in the middle. Both Presidents loved Archie, and Archie loved both Presidents, but both Presidents now hated each other. I hate it when people I like bad-mouth someone I like. It's a no-win position. TR kept ripping Taft in the papers and Taft started to complain to Archie about TR. The feuding leaders put Archie in the awkward middle.

Early in 1912, Butt was having some health issues and asked Taft for a leave of absence. Taft said yes and encouraged Butt to go to Europe and get away from politics for a while. Taft even apologized, saying "I hope I have not added to your troubles in any way."

Butt, who had never married, took a tour of Europe and loved it all. Near the end he wrote a letter to Taft saying that he "had met a woman in London who might be that someone special."

Two days later Archie boarded a big ship at Southampton, England bound for New York; an unsinkable tub called the *Titanic*.

Archie Butt's body was never found. President Taft was the eulogist at a service for Archie with 1,500 people in attendance, and the big man broke down a couple of times giving the talk.

50
The One-Term Pledge and the Six-Year Term

Wilson was annoyed to learn in the middle of the campaign that the Democratic Party had pledged their candidate, whoever it might be, to one term. The campaign platform read that "we urge the adoption of an amendment to the Constitution making the President of the United States ineligible for reelection and we pledge the candidate of this Convention to this principle."

When Wilson won the nomination he told the party to stop bringing that up and asserted that he was not obliged to honor it. So that pledge, while technically still in the platform, was little mentioned after the Convention, and the Republicans did not make political trouble with it in 1916 when Wilson was up for reelection.

The Democratic Party had for the past two years, from 1910-1912, been advocating the one-term six-year presidency. Too much energy was wasted on campaigning for the next election. Each President should serve one term and concentrate on his work for those six years.

The six-year one-term Presidency is still occasionally discussed seriously today. I see the merits, but then again, maybe it's good that the President is answerable to the people after merely four years.

In 1912, at the height of the Presidential campaign, the United States Senate and the House of Representatives actually passed bills recommending an amendment to the Constitution for a one term presidency of six years. Many Democrats, including the great William Jennings Bryan, urged candidate Wilson to commit to 1-6 before Election Day. Bryan not only asked President-elect Wilson to abide by it, he asked Wilson to push for it. Wilson just said no to 1-6. Even if he had ever one time thought it was a great idea, it certainly isn't likely to seem like a great idea to any President-elect. The whole political game is power. It's against human nature to ask anyone to voluntarily relinquish power. That amendment idea will always have support, but only from those who aren't about to have to abide by it.

There is little doubt, that if president-elect Woodrow Wilson had advocated the amendment to create a one-term six-year presidency, it would have been drafted, passed and ratified before the end of 1913, and the history of the United States would have been an entirely different story. It is another instance of the power of the individual upon history.

51
Ellen Wilson's Bill – August 6, 1914

Two days after Germany started a war in Europe, the First Lady passed away. It was a sad day in America. Ellen Wilson had been sick with kidney disease for almost a full year and she died in the Executive Mansion on August 6, 1914.

For more than a year Eleanor Wilson had advocated the improvement of slum conditions in the cities. Many thought she cared about the plight of the city poor more than the President did. Ellen was inherently shy, and stayed away from photographers and microphones. But for the sake of the suffering slum dwellers she came out of her shell and campaigned.

Ellen's influence on many influential friends of Woodrow had led to a Congressional bill to federal-fund slum relief. In the spring of 1914 this became known around Washington as "Ellen Wilson's Bill."

Ellie's Bill was stuck in the mud all spring and into the summer. When word reached Capitol Hill that Ellen Wilson had only days to live, Congress sprang into action so that news of the bill's passage could reach her deathbed before she passed. Ellen Wilson died knowing that she had, in at least one way, left the world a better place for her having been on it, which is all anyone can hope for in their lifetime.

Dying Ellen told her close friend, Doctor Grayson to tell Woodrow to marry again soon. She wanted him to be happy. Doctor Grayson read a prepared statement to the press announcing her death. Even though his voice did not falter, Grayson had tears streaming down his face. She was only 54.

Odd that this tragedy is so little remembered in American History. I can't imagine how sad I would feel if the First Lady died, no matter who she was. It's never happened in my lifetime.

52

Germany Bombs Maine – February 2, 1915

A German soldier disguised as a civilian got on a train in Boston with two suitcases. One case had a German army uniform in it; the other contained a fist full of dynamite. He travelled to Vanceboro, Maine and checked into the Mountain Moose Hotel, the only hotel in town. Vanceboro was at the border with Canada. Across the St Croix River was St. Croix, New Brunswick.

The soldier switched to full uniform, put the suitcase on the railroad bridge that separates the two countries, lit it with a cigar on a three minute fuse and then ran away like Tim McVeigh.

The blast damaged the bridge, but did not bring it down. It smashed windows in both St. Croix and Vanceboro. No one was hurt, and the man was caught and tried in Boston. The Vanceboro Bridge Incident worsened U.S.-German tensions. The bomber ended up in an insane asylum after the war.

This is certainly one of the least known, yet most interesting stories out of WWI. For a bomb that only broke a few windows, it certainly had a lot of impact. Germany was not at war with America, but was openly trying to attack American industry and infrastructure.

It seems in retrospect that WWI was still a bit young (only six months old) for Germany to risk antagonizing America into perhaps entering the war with such blatant sabotage. But to a German person in February 1915, the war had been dragging on an interminable six months and it was time for more drastic action.

U.S. production and export of war materials quadrupled in 1915. So the German spy ring led by Franz Von Papen had the okay from upstairs to attack and destroy any militarily useful target. German pride had taken enough and wanted to let North America know that it could not continue supplying the enemy with impunity. The German spy ring never thought of attacking soft civilian targets. Not even Huns would be so cruel and as cowardly at the same time.

The boss man who arranged the bombing of the Vanceboro Bridge was tried and sentenced to death at Nuremburg, but not for the incident at Vanceboro Bridge. Franz von Papen had been one of the political leaders of Nazi Germany, and for that he swung in 1946. Back in 1915 Big Papi was a rising star running spy rings.

Germany did not do itself any favors here. The bridge was out for about 10 days, but America was aroused to new anger; a diplomatic disaster for Germany.

A more detailed account now.

The actual operative who placed the bomb on the Bridge was a man named Verner Horn. He arrived in Vanceboro and immediately aroused suspicion by hanging around the bridge, taking measurements, keeping charts on the trains and acting suspicious - like an obvious bad-guy comic book character. Three citizen complaints led the Vanceboro police to take him into custody where he insisted he was only a Danish farmer looking to buy property in the area and he was scouting the countryside for places he might be interested in. They let him go because they couldn't charge him with anything.

Verner Horn hung around Vanceboro for three days trying to act normal. On the night of February 1, 1915 there was a snowstorm so bad that even the Abominable Snow Monster stayed inside for the night. It was 20 below zero. You might think I'm exaggerating. All right. I am. It was 30 below without the wind chill factor. In that part of Maine, not even a huge story for February. Verner Horn brought his suitcase to the Bridge and was about to light a 15 minute fuse when a train came by. Then another one stopped him in the middle of trying to light it only 12 minutes later. Horn wanted to destroy the bridge but did not want to cause a train crash with civilian casualties, so he shortened the fuse to three minutes, lit a cigar under his army coat and lit the fuse. It was 1:17 a.m. February 7, 1915. Verner was running back to the hotel when his bomb went off.

Horn changed clothes again somewhere along the way like Clark Kent and walked into the Hotel as if nothing had happened. Then he took a seat and started reading the paper like it was a day like any other. Seems a lot of guests were in shock that a huge bomb had gone off in town somewhere and here's the officially tabbed to be suspicious guy reading the paper in the middle of the room in the middle of the night casually saying, "Bomb? What bomb? I didn't hear any bomb."

And why did Horn switch to a German uniform before he set off the bomb? You would think he would want to wear anything but that when doing such a thing.

Because he didn't want to be executed as a spy if caught.

The cops closed in on the Mountain Moose and had Horn in hooks before breakfast.

Technically he had placed the bomb on the Canadian side of the bridge, but the Americans had him in custody. The Canadians wanted him extradited, but the Maine-iacs wanted to keep him. For a few hours the Americans didn't know what to charge him with in order to hold him. They decided to charge Vern with 200 misdemeanors for malicious destruction of property - the 200 plus windows in Vanceboro that his dumb bomb had blown out. Not that specious a charge, either. A lot of townspeople had suffered from the windowless cold in a blizzard, and Horn had some frostbite for his troubles too. That was good enough until the Feds could organize charges against him for transporting explosives on a passenger train. For that he was tried in Boston and sentenced to 10 years in a Federal prison in Georgia where he was eventually deemed insane.

No doubt Horn had never regained his sanity after experiencing how cold it can get in Maine.

53
The Sussex and the Sussex Pledge – March 1916

One of the most famous composers in the world in Woodrow Wilson's time was a Spaniard named Enrique "Ricky" Granados. He was also a famous painter.

One of the Rick's operas was so renowned that he was paid good money to come to America in February 1916 for a performance in New York City. That show went so well that President Wilson invited Granados to perform it in March at the White House. After the private screening, Granados dined with the President and his second wife, Edith Bolling Wilson. It was a delightful evening for all. When Granados said good-bye, President Wilson shook Enrique's hand warmly with two of his own and said, "That was fabulous. Thank you for sharing your gift with us. Have a pleasant journey, sir, and do write me when you get back to Spain."

Granados missed his non-stop cruise back to Spain because he had to step into a New York City studio to cut a vinyl record of his great opus. The detour put him instead on a ship to England, where he then transferred to a ferry across the channel bound for Dieppe France. From there he would catch a train across the plain to Spain.

The ferry *Sussex* made this run from Fokkaker, England to Dieppe on a daily basis and the weather on the afternoon of March 24, 1916 was clear.

Enrique was in the front portion of the ship talking with a Greek naval officer on leave named Spiro Tsakos, whose account of what happened next was later published in newspapers worldwide. Spiro had just convinced Enrique to take his cello out of its case and give a free concert for his many admirers traveling in boredom on the ferry ride.

Just as Granados was about to strike up the first note for the little circle of lucky fans, a German torpedo smashed into the side of the front portion of the ship. The entire bow was removed. Spiro spiraled into the sky. Enrique Granados, his wife, and the rest of the audience near the front were hurled through the cold spring air and down in the water. Some were dead, and others were suddenly swimming for their lives. Lifeboats were dropped. Enrique and Spiro managed to climb into one. Enrique heard the calls of his wife in the water and dove in from the lifeboat to rescue her. But his heroic deed was for naught. They both drowned. Spiro Tsakos told/sold this sad story to the world.

U-29 had torpedoed what it thought was a minelayer. But the *Sussex* only had civilians on board. Almost 50 people were killed. 25 Americans were reportedly injured, two seriously. It's odd that not one of the fatalities was American.

What was also seriously hurt was America's feelings, or at least Mr. Wilson's. Woodrow was insulted and enraged. The President went before Congress on April 19, 1916 and, in an emotional speech (he had to hold back tears when he mentioned "my good friend Enrique"), demanded that Germany stop sinking passenger ships, and show more restraint when sinking ships of neutral nations. If Germany would not behave, the United States would break diplomatic relations. Wilson didn't threaten any actual military retaliation, just the serious pledge that "we won't talk to you ever again." That usually leads to war. Wilson was painting himself and his country in a corner because he'd become attached to a pop celebrity and became emotional when his rock star friend died. He was pushing America into war over an incident in which not one American had been killed. Wilson turned the Sussex into a second Lusitania.

Germany wanted to keep the U.S. out of the war, and the Kaiser was embarrassed, as was the U-boat captain for the tragedy. Germany was genuinely ashamed of this stinking sinking. The Germans made an official announcement that it would cease its infamous "unrestricted submarine warfare" policy. Wilson's threat that America would stop talking to Germany had done the trick. By not technically threatening force in response, Wilson was now still able to campaign in the fall for re-election as the man "who kept us out of war." Thus, Woodrow could run on two tracks, both as the candidate for preparedness, but also as a candidate for peace.

But threats are almost as dangerous as deeds because the time may come when you have to back them up. Wilson's belligerent threat to break diplomatic relations almost led the United States needlessly and directly into war in 1916 in the first place. It definitely indirectly led the U.S. into war in 1917 by shortening the size of the next step towards it.

54

Black Tom Explosion – July 30, 1916

One of the worst terrorist attacks ever to take place on United States soil occurred on July 30 1916 at Bayonne, NJ, less than one mile from the location of the World Trade Center tragedy of 2001.

The munitions dump at Bayonne went up in an explosion that was equivalent to an earthquake of 5.2 on the Richter Scale.

The Germans did it. It was sabotage. The Kaiser had upped the ante from the incident at Vanceboro Bridge. The United States had been supplying Germany's enemies with munitions, and Germany answered back. It happened at 2:08 a.m. The shock from the blast was felt in Philadelphia! Windows all over Manhattan were shattered. People came out of their buildings in New York staggering amongst the broken glass trying to figure out what the hell was going on. Pieces of shrapnel were embedded into the Statue of Liberty.

The national reaction was cautious. The USA was still at peace and wanted to stay that way. So the tendency was to presume that it was an accident until proven otherwise. The Germans got the Bayonne benefit of the doubt. The Spaniards could have used the same tolerant break when the USS *Maine* exploded in Havana 18 years previously.

It wasn't until 1953 that the Germans finally admitted that they blew up the Bayonne munitions dump and agreed to pay an indemnity. It was a token gesture considering the billions the USA had already poured into the rebuilding of Germany by 1953.

55

U-53 Drops in Unannounced on Newport, RI – October 7, 1916

Early in the morning on October 7, 1916, the German submarine *U-53*, with Hans Rose as commander, appeared suddenly at the docks of the U.S. Naval Base at Newport Rhode Island. The Hun-sub had not been invited.

The United States was not at war with Germany, but it certainly was siding with the British. It's unclear exactly what motivated Rose to drop in on Newport without an invitation. This U-boat was a new boat on its first action cruise. 53's mission was more to protect a certain big German raider than to go after British shipping, but when it heard that the raider it was after had already been dunked by British naval artillery, it decided that it had the time to drop in on Newport before going back to work.

Professional military courtesy kicked in and the U.S. Navy acted quite nice about it. Rose actually boarded and toured the cruiser *USS Birmingham.* And U.S. Admiral John David, plus his wife and daughter, took a guided tour of the *U-53*.

Meanwhile, the e-mails were going back and forth between Newport and Washington. Crusty old U.S. Admiral Teevy broke up the party when he stepped on the *53* and handed Rose a note that if the sub did not leave Newport within two hours, 21 minutes, the American government would have no choice but to intern ship & crew for the duration of the war. Rose asked why the odd number of 2:21, and Teevy said, "It's now 2:20."

Hans Rose and his *U-53* got out of Newport and went back to work. Rose waited in ambush two miles from Nantucket Light and torpedoed three British cargo ships. U.S. destroyers were nearby during all these attacks, but could do nothing. The United States was neutral.

U-53 cornered a British liner and then allowed U.S. destroyers to save all the crew and passengers before sinking it. The U.S. Navy now looked like it was almost taking sides with the Germans against the British. This

German U-boat socializes with the Americans at the Newport Yacht Club, then the next day sinks three British ships while U.S. destroyers watch the whole thing and assists the Germans in evacuating civilians on a fourth ship, thus avoiding any atrocity at sea for the Kaiser. There was a lot of anti-American anger in Britain over this Newport affair.

It was just an accident of factors and timing. Naval people can't help but respect each other. They have the job in common, which binds them almost as much as enmity divides them. So it's not tough to picture the brass at Newport excited with curiosity to see a German U-boat appear out their window. The guys in Washington weren't so dazzled so they ordered *53* out. Then the bad night at Nantucket Light.

Hans may have been secretly looking around Newport in a military intelligence info-trip frame of mind while pretending to want to see the Tennis Museum. If he was working for the Kaiser in this way, the Rose ruse backfired.

The main result of this surprise visit to Newport was to wake up the United States to the vulnerability of every city and naval facility on the Atlantic coast. Tensions were already high between the Kaiser and the President when this visit hit the newspapers of America. The mood of the Administration and the Congress was suddenly for more naval appropriations "on the double." Germany paid in the Atlantic in 1918 for waking up the sleeping sea-hawks of America in 1916.

Hans Rose kept sinking ships right to the last days of WWI. He survived WWI as one of the great underwater sea captains of all time. Rose published his memoirs in 1932, called *Down You Go!*

56
The Forgotten Handshake of 1916

The election results of November 1916 between Democrat Woodrow Wilson and Republican Charles Evans Hughes were very close. It was two days past election night before the tally was officially figured for California. Whichever man took California would win it all. It was Wilson in California by only 3,373 votes.

Republican Chuck Hughes lost California and the Election of 1916 partly because of a political blunder, the infamous "forgotten handshake" he failed to extend to California Governor Hiram Johnson.

Late in the campaign Hughes stayed overnight at a hotel where Governor Johnson, a popular progressive Republican well-known to the entire country, was also staying. Hughes could have stopped by and just shook Johnson's hand and then apologized for needing to turn in early. But by neglecting to visit Johnson two flights down, Hughes created a story the press could have fun with. They didn't miss the chance and made a big deal out of nothing.

People bought it; that the forgotten handshake was a big insult to the beloved Hiram Johnson. The progressives in California got mad at Hughes, and a few thousand votes went out the hotel window.

This social snub probably changed the entire course of world history. The years 1916-1921 were crucial ones for the entire world and America's role in it. What would Hughes have done with the challenges that later faced Wilson? How much say would Republican Teddy Roosevelt have commanded in these years from behind the scenes?

57

Dan Dailey –
"Nobody Lives Forever!" - 1918

Dan Dailey was brave. How brave was he? He was so brave he won the Congressional Medal of Honor twice; first in Peking, then in Haiti. Then he won the Navy Cross on the Western Front. Looking at pictures of this guy, it makes sense that he liked to fight. Daly led a charge out of a trench with a call that became a legend:

"For Chrissakes boys, let's go! Nobody lives forever!"

If I was in the trench looking up at him saying that to me and seeing bullets tearing holes in his hat, I would just stay where I was.

The story later was changed to take the "Christ" out of what Dano said. It got watered down to "For Pete's sake."

58

Frank Luke, The Arizona Balloon Buster - 1918

Lt. Frank Luke Jr., 'The Arizona Balloon Buster' was the first U.S. airman to receive the Congressional Medal of Honor. Luke was killed in action while piloting a British SPAD on September 29, 1918 at Murvaux on the Meuse-Argonne front. At the time of his death Frank Luke was the reigning ace of the USA in WWI.

Lieutenant Luke's specialty was shooting up German dirigibles. Five balloons could make an Ace just as legitimately as five Fokkers. You might think that shooting balloon shouldn't count the same as shooting down a fighter plane, but the zeppelins were heavily guarded both in the air and on the ground. They had anti-aircraft around them plus a CAP (combat air patrol). Taking out balloons was, in fact, especially risky work. They blew up with a fury, and the flames and gasses could take the attacking plane down.

Luke was an eccentric athletic blonde introvert from Arizona. He didn't say much and when he did speak, it was usually an irritating brag. Frank was a great pilot and he knew it. Plus he kept to himself. Most of the other air-heads didn't like Luke very much. He was an enigma, a former bare-knuckles boxer who wrote to his mom, "you should not worry about me because the air corps is the safest place on the entire battlefront." It makes no sense, but that's what he wrote.

Luke would be on the ground and see a German fighter overhead and then say to anyone nearby, "It would be a piece of cake for me to take that guy out." It was irritating. But he meant it and he planned on backing it up. The guy was nuts.

For two weeks in mid-September 1918 Lt. Luke went on attack missions against zeppelins at anchor in German-held French territory. Luke shot down ten balloons in two weeks and returned home with his SPAD-25 shot to ribbons almost every time. Luke became famous. Ten balloons was big time stuff. He had a few plane kills from regular dogfights too.

But Luke's luck ran out of fuel on September 29, 1918. This account is based on a sworn affidavit from seven townspeople from the town of Murvaux who witnessed the last battle of the Arizona Balloon Buster.

Luke was attacking one anchored zeppelin with an entire squadron of German Fokkers on his tail. He went into a loop, straightened out and made a run for a second balloon. With the Germans still shooting at his tail he destroyed the second balloon. Luke pulled up and turned towards another target but caught a round in the shoulder and went into a twirling spin towards the ground.

Halfway to impact, Luke got a hold of himself, straightened out the plane and made for the town of Murvaux. There were no balloons there so he strafed German infantry positions, killing six soldiers and wounding at least 20 others.

Luke landed his damaged plane in a field, got out of the cockpit and walked briskly towards a nearby stream to treat his wound and get a drink. He spotted a German patrol heading his way about 200 feet away. He could have saved his life and surrendered, but Lt. Luke immediately went for his pistol and began shooting at the Germans before they had even taken a warning aim at him. The Germans returned fire as a unit and Luke took one square in the chest.

Luke was the real deal. It's nice to know that people like that existed and got the chance to do what they could do in time of danger. I'm not sticking up for war, but it does create greatness in some people.

The body of the American Top Gun Luke was stripped by the poverty-stricken German soldiers. His body was tossed on a wagon where it sat for an afternoon. Several French townspeople tried to at least get a blanket to cover up his body, but were blocked by German officers.

Lt. Luke won the Medal of Honor. Pilot Eddie Rickenbacker surpassed him in combat victories and finished as the number one Ace in World War I.

59
Pressie Bush Saves General Pershing's Life - 1918

Late in 1918, the *New Haven Journal-Courier* ran a page-one story about a local boy who made hero in France. The soldier had saved the lives of Generals Foch, Pershing and Haig by picking up a live grenade and hurling it away in the nick of time. The Allies practically gave him a parade. Foch pinned the highest medal in France on him, the Napoleon Cross. That soldier was none other than Prescott Bush, the father of the 41st President of the United States.

Problem was…the heroic story wasn't true. Private "Pressie" Bush had written his father a humorous letter from France about how he was saving the world single-handedly. The father laughed at the dry wit, and left the letter lying around. Prescott's mom Dorothy picked it up and, missing the joke, cried with joy. Then she gave the letter to the local Connecticut newspaper. Then it got picked up by other larger newspapers. This fantasy story he made up to kill the boredom was banner headlines in the New Haven newspaper. It was an embarrassing nightmare for the Bushes.

The Bush family straightened things out and the newspapers had to print retractions.

In 1972 my friend wrote a letter to the *South Boston Tribune* about a local teen-ager who just won a scholarship to MIT. The kid was the least academically minded person we all knew and the *Tribune* printed it. We laughed till we cried. They even included the boy's picture.

60
Death of Two Roosevelts – 1918, 1919

In July of 1918, a 23-year old pilot named Quentin Roosevelt from New York was stationed at Toul France. On July 10th Quentin got his first kill, bagging a German Fokker biplane. On July 14 Captain Roosevelt with three other American planes ran into a 'gaggle of Fokkers.' It was seven Fokkers against four Yanks.

Three Fokkers jumped Quentin and he took one through the head. Quentin Roosevelt, the son of former President Theodore Roosevelt was dead.

When the Germans identified the dead pilot they gave him the royal treatment. Quentin Roosevelt got a burial worthy of a German general; and this in the middle of an active war front. One thousand German troops stood at attention as QR's coffin was lowered into a grave at Toul. A proclamation was read and a band played a sad tune.

An American POW witnessed the Roosevelt funeral.

The Germans explained to the curious American POW that they were honoring Quentin because he was a gallant pilot and because he was the son of a great man. The first part probably meant little on its own, but the Germans really did think of TR as a great man. TR stood for the same set of martial values as Germany.

Six months later, former President Theodore Roosevelt died suddenly at his home in Oyster Bay Long Island at 4:00 a.m. on January 6, 1919.

Since he went as an explorer to the jungles of South America, Roosevelt had been battling a number of illnesses directly or indirectly caused by the fever he caught there. He had recently spent several days at the Roosevelt Hospital. Not many people get treated in a hospital named after them.

On January 5 Theodore Roosevelt wrote an article for a Cincinnati newspaper and then went to bed. His long time black servant James Otis looked in on him in the middle of the night and became alarmed by Teddy's irregular breathing. James summoned a nurse who summoned a doctor who pronounced him dead at 4:40 a.m. His last words were, "James, please turn out that light."

After a violent lifetime, this irrepressible man died peacefully in his sleep from a blood clot in his lungs.

Had he lived, TR might easily have been the Republican Nominee for President in 1920, and he would have won the White House if he had been nominated. Roosevelt had made it clear that he would not actively seek the nomination, but would accept if drafted. So obviously you can use your imagination on how things would have been different in the national story if TR had held on physically and become President instead of Harding. He might have surprised everyone and fought for America's entry into the League of Nations, but that's an open question to say the least.

On January 6 President Wilson was on a train in Italy as it pulled to a stop at a mountain resort. Witnesses saw Wilson read a telegram announcing the death of his arch-rival. His face went from shock, to passing sadness, then finished in a satisfied glow of final victory. It wasn't Wilson's finest moment, and he probably didn't realize that people were watching him through the window amidst all the smoke and commotion of the train station.

TR lost another son in a World War, this time the Second one. Theodore Roosevelt Jr. died in Normandy in 1944.

61
Albert Read and the NC-4 – May 1919

Who was the first person to fly the Atlantic? It wasn't Charles Lindbergh.

In May of 1919, the world became a smaller place. Three U.S. Navy flying boats called NC's (Navy Craft) were ordered to fly the Atlantic Ocean to Europe. Just do it. That's an order. It had never been done before. The initiative came from the United States Navy; not from private pilots with a dream, or in search of prize money.

One of the three NC's made it across. The others had to land in the water.

The historic bird was named NC-4, commanded by Albert Read. He and his four-man crew were the first to fly across the Atlantic Ocean. The route was well marked by friendly ships placed at intervals giving helpful light, and reassurance against death. NC-4 left Newfoundland and landed at Long Island for the big hop. NC-4 made it safely to the Azores non-stop. There were a few scary moments along the way but the U.S. Navy had done it. After a short rest and refueling, the biplane finished the trip by landing in Portugal. There was a global celebration.

The breakthrough of cross-ocean flight had long-term national security implications for the United States. The oceans had protected the USA since the time of Washington. The Read NC-4 flight warned of a not too distant future when oceans could no longer guarantee homeland safety. If U.S. NC4 could do it in one direction, the Germans or the British could attack America by air from the other.

Later that year of 1919 the inter-continent trip was made for the first time non-stop. The heroes this time were John Alcock and his co-pilot Lieutenant Arthur Brown. Their plane, *The Crazy World of Arthur Brown* crossed the Atlantic at one jump a full eight years before the Spirit of St. Louis.

The Lindbergh flight deserves plenty of glory, but it has

hogged it all unfairly; and the just as historic (and in my opinion, more so) flight of NC4 has none. It's all about media hype. Lindbergh was simply the first to fly it solo, which is hardly much more important than the first cross ocean flight, period. It was as if some solo astronaut landed on the moon in 2015 and somehow buried forever, the great event of the first landing on the moon in 1969, just because that was made by a three-man crew.

62
<u>Baby Ruth – 1904 & 1920</u>

Many history books mention the fun fact that the candy bar Baby Ruth was named after the daughter of President Cleveland, supposedly debunking the popular misconception that the bar was named after the greatest baseball player, Babe Ruth.

But was the Baby Ruth bar really named after Ruth Cleveland? Certainly the company that made the chocolate bar insisted on this and Nestle's Inc. still tells that story.

Let's look at the facts. Ruth Cleveland was born in 1891 when Cleveland was not in office, and she died young in 1904. The Baby Ruth candy bar was introduced in 1920. Is it logical that a baby-name candy bar would be named after a teenager that died tragically 16 years earlier in order to honor President Cleveland 12 years after he passed away?

The New York Yankees purchased the contract of Babe Ruth in 1920. What a coincidence that a candy bar named Baby Ruth just happened to hit the streets of New York City that same year.

George Herman "Babe" Ruth was a big guy, but wasn't big enough to swallow this story. The adult Mr. Ruth sued the candy company for using his name to sell candy bars. The company insisted that the candy bar had been named after Ruth Cleveland. The court ruled in favor of the company and called Ruth "a big baby" for filing the lawsuit.

You tell me who the Baby Ruth was named after.

If the Baby Ruth was named after Ruth Cleveland, than the Reggie bar of the early 1980's was named after the actor Reginald Owen.

63
Did Florence Harding Really Murder Her Husband? – August 1923

In the summer of 1923 President Warren Gameliel Harding decided that he had to get away from all the scandals plaguing his Administration, so he arranged a trip to Alaska with some of his friends. He would make conservation speeches up there and maybe get a little jump start on the campaign of 1924. WGH invited Commerce Secretary Herbert Hoover to join him on the trip, along with the usual crowd of hangers-on.

The expedition started in Tacoma Washington on July 3, and then went up to Fairbanks and back.

Harding was giving a speech in Seattle on July 27 before 60,000 cheering fans when he began to fail to speak his lines properly. His body began to shake and his papers fell to the ground. Hoover was sitting behind him and arranged the papers in proper order while Harding recovered just barely enough to finish his Seattle speech. Harding handlers cancelled the rest of the stops. He was scheduled to give three speeches a day at each of them.

Harding's doctor gave his President a close exam. Dr. Muzzey insisted that it was just food poisoning. Bad crabs in Vancouver had caught up with the President in Seattle.

But, another doctor looked at him and thought that Muzzey was looney. This doc decided that Harding had suffered a heart attack and needed emergency treatment.

One of the Cabinet members on the trip was Hugh Work. He had been a doctor before he went into politics, so his was the deciding vote among the three physicians. Work took a look at Harding and could not believe that Dr. Muzzey had ever said it was seafood poisoning. Harding had definitely suffered a heart attack.

Arriving in San Francisco, Warren G. checked in to the Palace Hotel. He never checked out. The maid screamed in horror when she found him dead. The heart attack diagnosis had been correct. Warren G Harding died on August 2, 1923 of a "coronary thrombosis." He was the third president to die in office from natural causes (Harrison & Taylor.)

The idea that Warren G. may have been poisoned came from a sensational book by Charles Means called *The Strange Death of President Harding*. It is a breathtaking read that implies that Florence Harding had the motive the means, and the opportunity to kill her husband the president. Warren was cheating on her repeatedly for many years and Florence usually prepared his meals. It was she who ordered that there be no autopsy. To tell you the truth, when I finished reading this spectacular book, I thought she did it. But apparently some killjoy wrote a recent book disproving this old wives tale. Then I read a review that challenged the debunker, so...

Either way, innocent or guilty, what matters is that a generation of Americans bought the theory for many years. It was very common conversation.

Harding definitely had a love child with a woman named Nan Britton, which gave Flo her motive.

Wikipedia, a source as reliable as an elderly alcoholic blues bass player, makes no mention of the fact that many people thought Florence Harding may have murdered her husband. The Means spirited book suggesting murder was a sensation. History has no right to bury it because it's creepy. Wiki mentions the newer book, Robert Ferrel's *The Strange Deaths of Warren G. Harding* (note the 's') while completely omitting the original book that the spin-off title was based on.

True or false, the fact of this widely believed and discussed tale is a significant part of American History and Means was a contemporary who was close to the story. And if one reviewer who debunked the Ferrel book as too debunker know-it-all, is worth anything, then we're right back to square one. Maybe she did it. He really humiliated her with his affairs and she was the one who made him president with her behind the scenes drive; a drive he lacked. She had motive, opportunity and Means. She was the one with him on his last day, giving him his medicine. Florence gave Warren G. the medicine he deserved.

64
"I Think I Can Swing It" – August 1923

Calvin Coolidge was at the old homestead at Plymouth, Vermont on the night of August 2, 1923. The Vice President of the USA was in the upstairs bedroom with Gracie when the sound of his father calling his name woke him up.

"Calvin, wake up son! Wake up! This is urgent!"

"It had darned well better be," grumbled the VP as he put on his night-robe and lit a candle.

The father's voice was trembling as he came up the stairs and announced, "Harding is dead, son." Then he entered the room and said with deliberate drama, "Or should I say, Harding is dead...Mr. President."

Calvin returned his father's stern stare and said with New England his voice, "Don't worry Dad, I think I can swing it."

The two political men dug up the family Bible and a copy of the U.S. Constitution. They read it closely to make sure there was no legal reason why the father, a legal magistrate, could not administer the oath. There was nothing in the Constitution about who could administer the oath and about where the oath had to be administered.

An emissary from Washington had arrived asking Coolidge to come to D.C. to take the oath, but father and son declined. They both agreed that it would not be wise or proper to go to Washington for this. The country would be two days without a President, and there was no reason that should be.

An hour later a little group of witnesses gathered at the Coolidge household, including Senator Dale who happened to be visiting.

And so, by gaslight in his father's living room at 2:27 a.m. on August 3, 1923, Coolidge became the only President sworn into office by a family member and the only president who took the oath in New England. There is an accurate drawing of the event, but no photos. After the 'so help me God' Calvin turned to his wife Gracie and hugged her. She had been shedding quiet tears through the ceremony. There were eight witnesses including one member of the U.S. Congress, James Thatch Hutt (Calvin only mentions Senator Dale in his memoirs, but another account says that Hutt was there).

Coolidge served without a Vice-President for the remaining 20 months of the Harding term. The USA has been somewhat lucky that every time it functioned without a Vice-President, the new sitting Prez remained alive. Tyler, Johnson, Arthur, and Teddy Roosevelt and then Coolidge were collectively veepless for all or a part of 22 years (1841-45, 1865-69, 1881-1885, and 1901-1905, 1923-1925). There was absolutely nothing in the Constitution about what to do if a VP succeeds a dead President and then dies too! We will never know how the USA would have solved that one! There was no official order of succession to the Presidency beyond the Vice President until 1947. And there was no provision to appoint a new VP until 1967 with the 25th Amendment.

65
Stanford University's First Shortstop

In 1890, Herbert Hoover took his life savings and used it to enroll in a new university. Mr. Leland Stanford had founded it. Herbert Hoover was the second young man to enroll in the university.

Stanford University's first baseball team had a starting shortstop named Herbie Hoover. He was also the business manager of the first Stanford football team. One book says he tried out for shortstop and didn't even make the team, so I'm going with starting shortstop.

Herb was a member of the first graduating class of Stanford University in 1895. That's how to start a school off with a bang; a future president.

Hoover met his Waterloo at Stanford. Lou Henry was from Waterloo, Iowa and she was, as he wrote to a friend, "cute and sweet, an unstoppable combination." With Iowa in common, they hit it off and later married. Sweet Lou was the only woman he ever loved, and the only woman he ever dated. Mr. Excitement, as usual.

After college Herb spent a couple of months in Hooverville, a station in life that would later be named after him. Herbert Hoover eventually became very, very rich. When he ran for President in 1932 he could not be bought.

The one thing I think people should realize about Herbert Hoover is that his hard work and initiative as head of the Belgian Relief Administration at the end of WWI saved millions of lives. His work with the BRA was so wonderful that President Wilson allowed him to help out in other countries, with U.S. support, including Russia. Hoover is only remembered for the Great Depression, but he was a truly great humanitarian. He is only remembered for the Depression, but he saved millions of lives and pitched in a great deal of his own money to help do so.

66
<u>The Death of Will Rogers –</u>
<u>August 15, 1935 – Pt. Barrow</u>

First of all, I love Will Rogers. And I was born 20 years after he died. I can only imagine how people felt about him when he lived, and then how badly they felt when he died.

Will Rogers, the greatest comedian of all time died in a plane crash on August 15, 1935.

Will Rogers was flying shotgun with Wiley Post, one of the most famous aviators of all time, when their little plane got lost in a fog and landed in a lagoon 13 miles south of Point Barrow Alaska. Point Barrow is the northernmost point in the United States. Some native Eskimos saw the nearly stranded plane and gave them directions to the little airstrip at Point Barrow. Will and Wiley thanked them and tried to get airborne again, but the plane lost power on take-off, plunging into the tundra and killing both great men.

Wiley Post was the first person to fly around the world. The two of them loved the adventure of flying and were planning a flight across Siberia in the near future. The crash of August 15 ended two careers in their prime.

I get choked up thinking about this event. There is no comedian today, nor has there been one in my lifetime, whose death could really shake up the entire nation. This witty home-spun friendly talkin' feller touched the lives and hearts of millions. His jokes were brilliant, funny, classy and poignant. He never told a vicious or a filthy joke. Although he tweaked the Republicans more than the Democrats, he was definitely even-handed compared to today's political wits who always have to have a one-sided bias. Rogers was the man who said "I do not belong to any organized political party. I'm a Democrat." The death of Will Rogers shook America. What John Lennon's assassination was to my era, the death of Rogers was to the 1930's. He also loaned out about everything he ever made to plain folk friends who were hurting, and he never got paid back except in reputation.

Today's greatest comedian might meet the President at

the White House Correspondents Dinner. Will Rogers actually consulted with Presidents. Men like Coolidge and Hoover wanted his company, wanted his input, wanted his help. He was everybody's friend; which is what a comedian should be, but only one in a million can be that great. Will Rogers was in a class by himself.

The Comedy Central channel conducted a poll of the 100 greatest stand-up comedians of all time. I was surprised at how much I agreed with it, and, yes, Moms Mabley should indeed be #3. But I knew they would make one glaring error. They wouldn't include Will Rogers.

You say he wasn't a stand-up comedian? Rogers made thousands of speeches where he told sharp, relevant, insightful jokes for 5, 10 or 90 minutes. He started out in the Zigfield Follies telling jokes while spinning a lasso. He did his comedy monologues on the radio for years and years and he spoke to countless groups live. He was definitely a stand-up comedian.

Rogers was also a newspaper columnist and movie star. He did so many things so well that it got lost along the way that he was doing insightful and edgy political stand-up humor while Mort Sahl and Lenny Bruce were still in diapers. Stand-up didn't start in the 1950's, as the Comedy Central channel would have us believe.

Will Rogers is my idol. I read books about him when I was a teen-ager and am still star struck by his legend. I still have trouble reading about that plane crash.

The movie where his son plays his late dad is excellent.

My Mount Rushmore of Stand-up Comedians has always been Will Rogers, Lenny Bruce, George Carlin and Bill Cosby. Now that Cosby has ruined his good name I'll have to replace him with someone else, but I just can't think of whom. Maybe I'll just put Rogers up there twice.

67

The Ludlow Amendment – 1935-38

Congressman Louis Ludlow rode the wave of anti-war isolationist fever when he proposed an astonishing amendment in 1935. The Ludlow Amendment would have made a United States declaration of war subject to a referendum by the voters!

A direct attack on U.S. soil would be exempted, but other than that it was to be a trip to the polls before U.S. troops moved. Roosevelt campaigned to stop the Ludlow Amendment and it lost in the House by a close vote. If FDR hadn't lobbied hard to stop it, it probably would have passed.

Isolationists everywhere praised the idea. *Good Housekeeping* magazine urged the people to write letters to their Congressmen supporting the amendment.

How would U.S. history have been different if Ludlow had become law? The Pearl Harbor attack probably still would have meant war. Korea would (I'm just guessing) have passed by a slight margin, but there may never have been a Vietnam. Ludlow probably would have stopped both Bush wars (1991 & 2003). If there was a Ludlow Law in 1860 the South would have seceded in peace.

Mr. Ludlow tried to push his bill through Congress for more than two years. The war by referendum amendment finally came to a vote in January 1938, helped by an isolationist reaction to the 1937 Japanese attack on the *Panay* in December 1937. The Ludlow amendment lost 209-188.

By 1938 a Gallup poll revealed that no less than 70% of American believed that the USA should never have entered The Great War of 1914-1918. There were anti-war rallies in the early thirties all over U.S. college campuses. In the spring of 1936 for example, 500,000 students at various colleges staged a strike for peace and carried banners that read "Scholarships, Not Battleships." Of course it never occurred to these people that peace movements are ignored by aggressors. 1930's lefties forever patted themselves on the back for being morally superior to anyone who favored a strong military. Same deal today.

68

The Only Two Men FDR Ever Screamed At

According to FDR's private secretary Grace Tulley, the only two men FDR ever screamed at were Joe Kennedy and Hap Arnold.

By the beginning of 1940 the American Ambassador to England, Joe Kennedy, had made himself very unpopular in London. Joseph hindered the friendship between Great Britain and the United States by managing to get just about everyone in London to hate him. Not exactly his job assignment. In addition to being uncouth and discourteous, which the Brits could have barely tried to forgive, Joe Kennedy blabbed out loud to anyone who cared to listen that Britain was going to lose the war with Germany, should sue for peace with Germany, and that America should stay out of it. Any of these three opinions would arouse any patriotic Briton to hate him, but all three was enough for people to develop an obsession about hating him.

FDR did not share these opinions. To have his Ambassador to England going around from one social club to the next, mouthing off about how Britain was going to lose the war, and to leave the club with people being restrained from going out after him to beat him up; all these scenes were bad news to FDR. In addition, Joe Kennedy was thinking of challenging FDR for the Presidency in November 1940.

It was always tense whenever Ambassador Kennedy visited the White House, but there was one time in particular, in the spring of 1940 that Grace overheard a most violent shouting match. She could only pick up snippets of the dialogue, but she said that they weren't merely arguing, they were downright screaming at each other.

When Joe Kennedy stormed out of the White House (and slammed the door), FDR would not tell Grace Tulley a word of what they argued about, but he did condemn Joe

Kennedy in nearly vulgar terms.

I'm just passing the story along. I don't hate Joe Kennedy.

The other guy that really got yelled at was Hap Arnold, the leader of the Army Air Force.

The United States had agreed after Munich to supply England and France with combat planes in 1939-40.

But Hap Arnold didn't like this plan. Arnold wanted to keep his best new planes plus U.S. advancements in warplane technology secret. In 1940 France and England both pleaded with America for these promised planes. They accepted that the USA was not going to intervene, but at least send us the planes. France desperately begged for planes as it was falling in May and June 1940.

In the emergency FDR authorized the shipping of several squadrons of U.S. fighter planes to France. But Arnold had cleverly obstructed these orders with administrative delays equivalent to the sabotaging of a direct order of strategic importance from the commander in chief.

When FDR got wind of what Arnold had been up to he called him into the Oval Office and gave him a brow-beating that HA surely remembered to his last day on earth.

Roosevelt yelled at Hap Arnold so you could hear it in Virginia. He told Arnold that he should be thankful his president was in a wheelchair otherwise "they'd settle it like men." The people of Europe were threatened with fascist invasion and, "my own commander in the air arm is making his own foreign policy behind my back. I cannot only fire you, I can tell it all to the *New York Times* and don't think I won't!"

Hap Arnold slithered out of the White House.

Two weeks later, orders were in the works to send France, Norway and Britain a total of 2,898 American fighters and bombers over the next 12 months. But the ink wasn't dry on the order sheets before it was too late. Hitler won his war too fast.

What if Arnold had taken the opposite approach and went out of his way to expedite the FDR declared policy after Munich to rush warplanes to Europe? France might have held on with more to fight with.

69
<u>Why Do They Yell "Geronimo!"?</u>

What did Geronimo yell when he jumped off a cliff? "Meeeeeeeeeeee!"

So why do people yell 'Geronimo!' when they jump from great heights? Was Geronimo famous for his high diving feats?

It started in 1940 at Fort Benning, Georgia. Green airborne trainees were preparing for their first real jump. The night before they all saw the movie *Geronimo*. The boys were sitting around before lights out, talking about tomorrow and about being scared. One guy named Chet Adenhart was something of the lovable, but nervous type and the guys teased him, reminding him that "some guys are so scared on their first jump they can't even remember their own name."

Adenhart told them, "I'll prove to you guys that I'm not scared. When I jump, I'll scream my name. I'll shout "Adenhart!, and then I'll jump."

No one thought much about it until the next day when Adenhart was at the green-lit open door. It was time. He gave a look back to the guys, and screamed "Geronimo!" as he jumped. The men behind him got the joke, roared laughing. Then each one of them yelled "Geronimo!" as he jumped.

The story made the rounds at Fort Benning and soon every rookie was yelling Geronimo on his first real jump. The tradition grew to include every jump and now it's just part of the American culture. Kids yell "Geronimo!" as they jump off a pier into a lake.

70
<u>Churchill in the Hurricane</u>

At one point during the late December 1941 Arcadia Conference in Washington, Churchill was physically worn out from all the hard travel and all the tough meetings. He collapsed in his hotel room and sent for a doctor. His British doc told him that he almost certainly had suffered a mild stroke and that he should go back to Britain at once. Churchill begged him to keep the whole thing a secret, because the conference was too important. The doctor agreed and Churchill merely admitted to all that he was quite fatigued. Ed Stettinius had a nice place in Palm Beach Florida and offered it to Churchill for a mid-Arcadia break and Winston said yes. There he was, the fat old political superstar, sun bathing on the Palm Beach like any other tourist for three days.

Churchill went back to Washington. He and FDR got along famously. Churchill liked to wheel the President around the White House while they talked. Churchill even let FDR do a lot of the talking, which was not easy for Churchill.

Churchill helped to light the National Tree on Christmas Eve and addressed a joint session of Congress on the day after Christmas. It was an emotional speech. I've heard large portions of it and it's great. My favorite part is when he warns Japan, "What kind of people do they think we are!" It's a question, but I'm going with the exclamation mark. He was angry, and it was perfect.

When it was finally time to leave, Churchill caught a ship to Bermuda and was supposed to catch another one back to England. But that was too dangerous, what with the prowling U-boats and all. So he took a big Boeing four-engine plane instead. Churchill was sound asleep while the pilot got lost in a fog and ended up flying over French territory where the Nazis could have easily Yammammotoed the old man. The pilot almost decided to land before he realized his error!

But that's not that half of it. When the Boeing found its bearings and headed back to England, the RAF sent up six

Hurricane fighters to shoot it down! It was unidentified and the only reason he survived was that there was a heavy fog and the RAF fighters couldn't find the "hostile" plane. Imagine if the RAF had shot down Winston Churchill's plane and killed the in-his-Prime Minister. It takes my breath away to think about it. The pilot who got lost over Nazi territory was an American. How sorry I would feel for the poor British pilot who shot down his wartime leader. I'm sure that guy would have ended up with a severe drinking problem.

71
<u>Ni Hao Ma!</u>

Nihau Island is one of the most westerly of the Hawaiian Islands. It is small. There were a few dozen farmers on Nihau in December of 1941. Nihau had no telephones, roads, or electricity. Japan "seized" it on December 7 and held on to it until December 14.

Here's how this bizarre tale happened.

A Japanese Mitsubishi Zero fighter from the second wave of the attack on Pearl Harbor became lost and crash landed in a Nihau field. The pilot was named Shigenori Nikikaichi. His Zero came to a stop within 30 feet of a startled Hawaiian named Hawila Kaleohano, a big guy who ran up to the plane and confronted the pilot. Hawila took the pilot's gun and map.

The natives on Nihau knew there was tension between Japan and the USA, but they had no knowledge of the attack on Pearl Harbor. There was a language barrier. A translator was needed and a woman soon arrived who spoke Japanese and Hawaiian. She spoke to Niki for a few minutes in Japanese and told the others that the pilot was friendly and not part of any hostile mission. He was way off course and it was all an accident.

The Hawaiians on Nihau relaxed and even held a party in honor of the downed Zero pilot in the early evening of December 7, 1941. They kept his gun, just to be safe, but it was all friendly.

But late that night the interpreter returned, this time with her husband. They were Nisei Japanese immigrants who were apparently still loyal to Japan. They had concealed guns. The three of them on cue lost their fake smiles and announced that they had the drop on the others. It was like an old black and white movie. "Arrite nobody move and no one gets hurt!"

Through his Hawaiian traitor-interpreters Shigenori, who now had his own gun back, told them all proudly about the attack on Pearl Harbor. His two pals ordered the others to help this pilot get back to Japan. The pro-Axis trio took two hostages and threatened to kill them if the U.S.

government didn't help the pilot escape back to Japan. The other Hawaiians fled in all directions.

For the next several days Nihau, a United States Hawaiian island, was held by one Japanese pilot and two quislings with three pistols.

On December 13, the two hostages rebelled and fought it out with the pilot and the Japanese-Hawaiian couple. The husband traitor died from a fairly large stone to the head. The man who subdued the traitor was the same man who had taken in the pilot in the beginning, Mr. Kaleohano. He received two bullet wounds in the fight and survived. Kaleohano is one of the first real American heroes of WWII. The pilot and the woman surrendered. Nikikaichi was on the mainland in chains by December 15. But for a week, Nihau, Hawaii had actually been in Japanese hands.

The story might be fluff except for one serious thing. The dramatic little story became sensationally popular in America. The behavior of the Nisei traitors became part of the national mind-set, especially in Hawaii and on the West Coast. The Nihau incident contributed materially to the decision to intern Japanese-Americans during WWII. Most Americas at the time presumed that this was what the country was up against, as far as Nisei were concerned. This was probably the only real overt act of disloyalty in America by a Japanese-American. That woman and her husband helped set off the reactionary backlash that was the internment camps.

Ni Hao means hello in Chinese, and I can write it in Chinese lettering. Add the "ma" and it's a question, as in "how are ya?" No doubt the name Nihau is a reference to the Chinese greeting.

72

Surcouf – February 18, 1942

In February 1942, the biggest submarine in the world was the *Surcouf*, the pride of the French Navy, which had swallowed its pride. Super-sub had two eight-inch deck guns. Most WWII subs had one five-inch deck gun. *Surcouf* was cruising towards the Pacific to protect Fiji and New Caledonia for Free France. The Surcouf would settle any mini-civil wars that might be going on between Vichy and Free France in the Pacific. After that, it would proceed on and help the Americans in the Pacific war with Japan.

But the *Surcouf* never made it to Fiji. Late in the night of February 18, near the eastern entrance to the Panama Canal, *Surcouf* was puttering along just under the waterline. A U.S. freighter passed over the submarine and scraped it bad. The *Surcouf* broke up.

The American merchantmen heard yelling in the water, but they thought they'd dusted a German U-boat and were under orders not to stop and pick up enemy survivors. All 103 Frenchmen perished. De Gaulle in Brazzaville was all busted up when he heard the *Surcouf* was all busted up. The *Surcouf* was his best military card. It was a sad event for the Allied war effort, not just for Free France.

One more downer.

A few feet of history and the U.S. freighter would have passed nearby harmlessly. Imagine if *Surcouf* had sunk a Japanese carrier in 1942 during the low point of U.S. fortunes. The whole situation would have changed for Free France. De Gaulle's boys would gain new status with all the Allies through one major action. The whole position of Free France at Yalta and Potsdam might have been different.

73
The Cruise of the Marblehead

On February 4, 1942, Japanese planes based on Celebes, attacked a small Allied task force north of Java (both locations located in today's Indonesia). There were three cruisers and eight destroyers in the task force. Cruiser *U.S.S. Houston* suffered damage that killed more than 50 sailors, but failed to sink it. The DD *Marblehead*, an old 1920 vintage "four-piper" destroyer, was also hit hard.

Japanese Nell bombers hit the *Marblehead* with a dozen direct hits. Dead and wounded were all about the *Marblehead*, fires raged, yet she floated. *Marblehead* was in the middle of an extreme turn trying to dodge the next attack when a bomb, a near miss, smashed up the steering gear and locked it in at an extreme turning position. *Marblehead* then spun around in tight circles for hours and hours all over the Java Sea like an insane ship that had lost its marbles. The chart of the *Marblehead*'s course of February 4, 1942 looks like a Slinky.

It took some clever use of accelerating at various speeds to guide the wounded warrior through the strait that separates Bali and Lombok Islands, and from there to Tijilatjap on the south coast of Java. "Tiji" was overcrowded with ships from all over the region fleeing the Japanese advance, including all the ships that had fled Singapore.

There wasn't any room at the inn for *Marblehead*, so it got some thin emergency repair at Tijilatjap and set out due west for the Indian Ocean with a bow-dip of scary proportions. *Marblehead* spun its way in circles across the East Indian Ocean and picked up a little bit of repair at Ceylon. Then it slinked its way to South Africa, and eventually limped into New York City after a crippled-creek cruise around the world of 16,000 miles and 17,000 spins. Some sailors went insane from vertigo. *Marblehead* was back in action in North African waters in 1943.

The ordeal of the *Marblehead* inspired the Navy to make two changes in the rule-book. First; from then on, captains should try some moderation when making turns to avoid bombs. No more maximum tight turns. Tight, yes, but 100% extreme turns should be avoided just in case a bomb was to freeze up the steering in a max position. A near miss could put a ship out of action as thoroughly as a direct hit (near misses were murder on steering).

The other *Marblehead*-inspired change was in Navy uniforms. From then on, no matter how hot it gets in the South Pacific, no more shorts and tank tops. Pants and shirts please. Many of the men on the *Marblehead* had suffered severe burns on the legs and shoulders that could have been minor burns at worst if they had not exposed so much skin.

74
Hooligan's Yacht Club

In the first half of the Battle of the Atlantic, the trying years, the USA accepted volunteer help from many sources. In early 1942, private yacht clubs all up and down the east coast offered Sam the use of hundreds of vessels for reconnaissance, shoreline patrol and anti-submarine duty.

These yachts were offered unconditionally. The Navy could stock them with their own people if they wanted, or the owners would provide a crew if asked. Or there could be a combination of the two.

If America had enough destroyers (DD's) and patrol craft (PC's) to start the war with, the yacht club offer would have been gratefully rejected. As it was, the Navy still hesitated.

So, the yacht club people went over the admiral's topsails and pleaded with the public to ask their Congresspersons to pressure the Navy to accept yacht club help.

The subject became national gossip. Should the Navy take these volunteer martini drinkers in? Could the amateur boaters really help against Raeder's pros? Would these rich folk flee at the sight of a U-boat instead of tracking it? Could America provide its own version of the Miracle at Dunkirk with every private vessel doing its small part in a large effort?

Eventually the Navy gave in and made America's yacht clubs part of the Naval Reserve. They became the "Coastal Patrol." Yachts sailed into Navy yards and picked up two sets of machine guns, one 300-lb depth charge, and a good radio.

Now the gossip switched to potential results. How many German U-boats would the yacht clubs sink? The yacht that sunk the most U-boats might even receive a special All-America's Cup Trophy.

The Coastal Patrol became known as the "Hooligan Navy." The Hooligans were quite active from Maine to Brownsville. The Hooligans, however, never destroyed or even frightened a single U-boat. The reverse was true. A U-boat shot up a yacht, and killed a few dozen private sailors. That was the extent of the action between U-boat and yacht.

But the Hooligans succeeded at the recon end. They set up a series of 16-square-mile boxes up and down the coast. It was the duty of each yacht to patrol one assigned square. Yachts spotted and reported the positions of many U-boats in 1942-3, and they no doubt served as a deterrent to U-boat activity.

The yacht fleet got the nickname Hooligan Navy, because with the war already siphoning off all the young men, it wasn't easy to find a crew for all these yachts. The Navy couldn't spare any sailors, and told the yacht clubs to lower their standard if that's what they had to do. The Navy wasn't going to check up on anyone's credentials, wink-wink. The rich boys scoured the waterfronts for the tough guys on the edge of society and they all went sailing together. Long John Silver sailed with Thurston Howell III. Some prisons gave certain model inmates a chance to join the yacht club in exchange for parole.

By the fall of 1943, the U.S. had enough destroyers, and the Hooligan's Navy disbanded.

The service of the Hooligans restored the good name of the yacht club set, and then some. That name had been tarnished earlier. During the first weeks of the war there had been a regatta race in Chesapeake Bay while U-boats sank merchant ships just outside the bay. When that story got around, the yacht set was embarrassed. Hooligan's Navy fixed that flat.

75

Man Overboard! – March 27, 1942

In mid-March 1942, a U.S. Navy task force gathered at Casco Bay Maine. The U.S. Maritime Academy stands active there today. When I had a stand-up gig there a few years ago, I never realized that there had been a time when I could have gazed out into that Casco Harbor and seen the battleship *U.S.S. Washington*, the aircraft carrier *Hornet*, plus a host of cruisers and destroyers.

The brand-new long-awaited *Washington* and *Hornet* were originally supposed to go to the Pacific theatre, but Churchill convinced FDR that the situation in Madagascar trumped the situation in the Pacific.

Huh? Madagascar?

The Germans and Japanese were allegedly planning a team invasion of Madagascar, the huge island located off the southeast coast of Africa. The British believed that if successful, the Axis occupation would hurt the entire war effort. The Allied supply line to the Persian Gulf and India would be cut off, and Axis partners could soon unite in the Middle East on their way to total Eurasian domination.

The Axis invasion threat was more of a cover story. The British really wanted to take Madagascar away from the Vichy French who controlled it. The British might even think about staying on in Madagascar after the war ended. So, there was a bit of a colonialist vs. colonialist power game going on there, disguised as an Allied answer to a real Axis threat.

After WWII ended, colonialism plummeted world-wide for three or four decades, but in 1942, Churchill didn't know that was going to be the aftermath. For all he knew, the British Empire might emerge after the war stronger than ever with new acquisitions added on. Like Madagascar, for example.

Churchill wasn't asking the USA to take over the defense of Madagascar. He was going to send British warships from the North Atlantic to east Africa. Winston was merely asking the United States to replace those departed UK warships in the Atlantic. Despite protests from some of his military chiefs, FDR agreed. He was always a "stop Germany first" guy. And he did not like to buck Churchill unless he felt adamant about something.

The Casco Bay, Maine task force was the first major U.S. Navy capital ship contribution to the European War. It was a big deal. Admiral John W. Wilcox was the head honcho on board flagship *Washington*.

On March 27, the task force ran into a storm at sea. It was a long terrible blizzard of ice, snow, and terrifying winds. In the middle of the worst of it, several men on the *Washington* spotted a body face down in the middle of the water drifting behind the ship.

"Man overboard!" went the cry throughout the battleship.

One witness saw one arm flailing and knew the man overboard was alive. All witnesses agreed that it was a bald guy. The *Washington* and two destroyers circled around looking for the cold swimmer, but in the driving snow and the high seas it was tough.

When the storm began to subside, the *Hornet* sent a plane off its deck to look for the downed seaman, but that plane never came back. So, a pilot was lost looking for the man overboard on the 100-to-1 chance they could bring him back on board alive.

The next day in calm and sunny seas, the *Washington* held a full muster to determine who was missing. It turned out that the man overboard was the commander of the battleship; the commander of the entire task force, John W. Wilcox! Everyone else (besides the downed pilot) was present and accounted for.

When at first no one had been able to find Wilcox, people presumed that, with his authority, Wilcox had given orders not to be disturbed while he consulted with Washington by radio, studied battle plans with important officers, or got a ten hour nap. So it took a while to realize that 'the big guy' was missing.

Some at first thought that Wilcox might have committed suicide. A couple of people had mentioned that Wilcox looked notably despondent when they talked to him during the storm. But, as more people who had recently seen him were interviewed, the conclusion became clear.

The man had been dreadfully seasick.

One story after another told of Wilcox looking "white as a ghost." Wilcox was a top notch Annapolis officer, but simply had not spent enough time at sea to get his sea legs. Wilcox had evidently leaned over to the rail to empty his lunch and he accidentally tumbled over while doubled over as the big ship took a big dip.

I feel bad for Wilcox. Not because he died, but because he got that seasick. I got seasick on a whale-watch off Cape Cod in 1979 and will never forget it as long as I land-lubber live.

76
<u>St. Paul's – May 15, 1944</u>

The big Allied meeting preparing final plans for D-Day took place at St Paul's School in London on May 15, 1944.

General Montgomery was the leading presenter at this great meeting. Everyone who was anyone in the days before OVERLORD was there; from Churchill to Tedder, to Bedell Smith, to Ike, to General Simpson. Patton and Alexander were there. Mick Jagger was even there.

Montgomery had made some very strict rules about tardiness. He had no tolerance for it. Anyone who was not present when the meeting started would not be allowed in. He made that extra clear. You've been warned. Guards were placed around the building so that anyone who arrived late would be denied entrance to the meeting.

So, Monty was in the middle of his talk with maps, emotional urgings, and strategic plans and there was a loud banging on the door behind him.

Monty ignored it. He'd made his rules.

The banging on the door got louder and more persistent and would not cease. Finally Monty stopped, went to the door to open it and who was there but General Patton in shiny, showy uniform. Patton walked in without a word and took a seat to hear the rest of the speech. You could hear a pin drop as Patton settled in while Monty held his pause button.

Monty did not say anything about it, and continued his talk.

77
<u>Chelsea Cota – Hero of Omaha – June 1944</u>

Norm Cota, the pride of Chelsea, MA, did his job well on Normandy beach. With bullets and bombs whizzing by, Cota personally went up and down the beach explaining to the terrified soldiers lying in the sand, one at a time:

"Look son, if you move up off this beach you are probably going to die. But if you stay here on this beach you are definitely going to die."

His leadership lifted entire regiments off the beach. The man had grown up in Chelsea, and he was not afraid of the Nazis. Coda had already experienced bullets whizzing by his ear when he went to the milk store as a teenager.

Rallying the scared troops wasn't enough for 'Stormin' Norman' Coda. He led by example, not just words. Coda climbed off the beach and marched personally a half-a-mile inland; a one-man invading army. There were no other troops with him or anywhere near him. He came back and told the others which way was clear - the one he had just done a reconnaissance in force all by himself.

And by the way, General Schwartzkoff's nickname of 'Stormin Norman' was a spin-off of General Coda's nickname.

Coda won all the decorations a soldier can win, short of the Medal of Honor. General Bradley also gave him a serious closed-door hollering lecture on needlessly risking his life when he'd do more for the cause by first making sure he stayed alive. The leadership talent at AAA-ball wasn't all that good at the time. Bradley wasn't even happy with who he had in the starting line-up. His bench was poor. Cool it Coda!

By 5:00 p.m., things had actually settled down at Omaha Beach. The famous slaughter had taken place in a short, fiery window. Casualty figures vary from source to source and method to method, so approximately 750 Americans died and 1,500 were wounded there in one Omaha afternoon.

Robert Mitchum plays Norm Coda in the movie *The Longest Day*. Cary Grant plays Rommel and does an amazing German accent.

.

78
Patton's Map

As their armies approached each other in 1944-45, the Soviets and Americans exchanged military observers. A handful of qualified Americans were on the Russian front taking notes and trying to draw lessons from what they saw. But the Russians treated the American observers rudely most of the time and did not give them the proper access to the battles or the logistical information they desired.

Patton wanted to study the Russian front and was insulted by the reports he heard coming out of the Russian front about the way his boys were being treated.

When a Russian delegation of observers came to visit Patton near Toul on September 16, he took off. He wasn't around when they showed up. Patton left them a special battle map to bring back to Russia. It told them nothing. A tourist map had more info on it. Patton changed the name of some of the places on the map. Nancy, for instance, was re-named Svetlana, and Moselle River was re-named Trotsky River. The Russian observers probably destroyed the map rather than bring it back to Stalin.

Sometimes I don't like Patton, but in cases like these, I love him. He was one of the only American leaders that "got it" about the Russians. He was one of the few to understand that their rudeness towards ambassadors was a test, and was indicative of a larger goal of international aggression. FDR and others allowed Stalin to be rude to American emissaries (as long as Stalin was nice to FDR whenever they met) and thought rudeness by proxy just a minor problem.

Rudeness is always indicative of a larger threat looming behind it. I wish FDR had handed Stalin a couple of his own "Patton's Maps."

79
The Boar War - 1944

Not everyone in Luxembourg was thrilled with the American liberators of late 1944. Not the Luxembourg game warden.

The Luxembourg Forest was rich with wild boar and trout-filled streams. With the food shortage facing the U.S. Army, the forest became a prime natural supply depot. The Luxembourg game warden told the Americans that the boars were protected. You can't kill the boars. The Americans said, "Watch this."

Bright and early the next morning, American planes patrolled the boar reserve and massacred the boars by machine gun. It was a mismatch - wild boars vs. P-51 Mustangs.

The game warden was sure wasting his time. These hardened soldiers were indifferent to *human* life by now. These animals weren't about to weep for those animals. The game warden lost the boar war, and the G.I.'s were more than happy to munch down a Double McBoar with cheese and Vichy French Fries.

80
<u>To Hell and Back - 1945</u>

During the battles in the Colmar Pocket a soldier named Audie Murphy won himself the Medal of Honor and lived to tell about it. Few do. Murphy lived and went on to become a famous American movie star. I never liked his movies very much because I thought he was very flat as an actor. I have since learned that he knew it. Murph said, "I acted with a handicap...no talent."

I used to think that the Audie Murphy story demonstrated that the gun is the great equalizer, and that this little guy probably wasn't so tough without his weapon. But, no. The more you read about him the badder he gets. The little guy talked like a librarian, but fought like a wounded lion with rabies. Long after the war was over Audie was charged with attempted murder for beating a guy nearly to death at a bar. The guy had probably written an article suggesting that Murphy wasn't so tough without a gun.

Murphy won his Medal as a result of his actions on January 26, 1945 at a bridge in the French town of Merdeville. It was a very cloudy day and the Germans were counter-attacking in a clearing in front of some woods. Murphy's battalion was falling back in disarray. Audie Murphy saw an American tank burning, but with a turret machine gun intact. He ordered his men to retreat into the woods. Murph then jumped up on the burning tank, grabbed the machine gun, and took on a couple of hundred Germans. He fought them single handedly, didn't get scratched, and killed at least 200 of them. All the while his tank should have blown up. The guy was nuts.

Many vehicles were burning and all the action made the Germans think that Murphy could not possibly be alone. There was confusion in the Germans lines. But still, the Germans kept coming. The heavy low clouds had prevented any air support. Murphy still seemed doomed after all he had done. But then, like a miracle, the clouds broke and the Allied fighter bombers could see everything. They began strafing and bombing up real close and the

Germans retreated. Next thing you know, there was Murphy, ashen-faced, climbing out of the tank and heading back to tell his men in the woods that everything was okay.

The man was indestructible.

Audie was also decorated for courage in several other engagements. Winning the Medal of Honor was just another day at the office for this lunatic.

Audie Murphy was killed in a plane crash in the 70's. His combat saga was made into a move called *To Heck and Back*. The DVD is in the mail heading to my house as I write this.

Incredibly, the movie actually did not do justice to the courage of the deed. It did not convey the length of time Murphy fought all alone, nor the certain death that was closing around him. It neglected the aspect of the cloud cover opening up to save him, which was key to winning the Medal of Honor. He thought he was facing certain death and a miraculous stroke of luck saved him.

Author's Note: If you want to get technical, the vehicle he jumped into was not a "tank" but it looks exactly like one to the non-military observer. It didn't have enough armor plating to classify as a tank, but was a smaller self-propelled gun that looks like a tank.

81
<u>The Pied Sniper of Hamelin –</u>
<u>March 1945</u>

This story really happened very near the old city of Hamelin, but let's just say it happened in Hamelin, the home of the famous Pied Piper.

A lone G.I. with his M1 at the ready was walking down a thin village road when out of a house poured more than 40 Germans. For a moment the American thought he was done for, but the 40 Germans put their hands up to surrender. 40 soldiers were surrendering to one private. The biggest fear of most German soldiers at this point was how to surrender without getting shot. And they especially preferred to surrender to the Americans, as opposed to the Russians.

So this one G.I. accepts his role and starts a three mile march back to his base with 50 Germans walking behind him, all happy to be out of the war. 10 more had trickled into the surrender line before he began his journey. As he walked along the road more and more Germans came out of the woodwork and joined the parade. By the time he got back to his regimental base camp, this one G.I. had more than 1,200 German POW's marching behind him! He was the Pied Sniper of Hamelin, leading these rats to captivity.

82
Saving Private Waters – Hammelburg – March 26-29, 1945

The U.S. Army had liberated Cabantuan POW camp in the Philippines in a spectacular raid on January 30, 1945. In March of 1945 General Patton decided he was not going to be outdone. He planned a daring raid 55 miles deep inside German lines to liberate the Allied troops of OFLAF 13, the German POW camp at Hammelburg.

The Hammelburg raid was a complete disaster and Patton had to admit it. He claimed after the war that it was his only major mistake. Patton claimed that if he had only assigned more forces to the raiding party, it would have succeeded. Yeah, of course. And if Washington had 3,000 more troops at Brandywine, he would have won there too.

Patton assigned 300 men and 57 fighting vehicles to the mission. All they had to do was fight their way 55 miles to the town of Hammelburg, and then turn and fight their way south to the training camp/prisoner of war camp the Nazis were running just south of the town. The armed column would then smash in the gates of the camp and liberate the jubilant prisoners. Then, with the entire region alerted to the intruders, Patton's raiders, with liberated men clinging to the sides of the vehicles, would fight their way back to American lines another 59 miles. Sounds like a plan. In a best case scenario it was going to be a brutal firefight on the way in, and an even rougher one coming back out.

Colonel Bruce "Baby Man" Baum was given the task of forcing his way to Hammelburg. As the leader of "Task Force Baum," he wondered why he was handed this mission when no other prisoner of war camps were to be liberated in advance. Why this one? Weren't these POW's close to liberation anyway?

It turns out that the only reason for the mission to Hammelburg was that Patton's son-in-law, Jack Waters, was one of the prisoners. Nepotism in action. Patton took care of his family. His daughter would see her beau soon, and people would die for the favor.

The column battled its way to Hammelburg and took some losses on the way. Tanks crashed through the gates of the camp and there was a battle. Prisoners came out in jubilation.

The column had now been through two phases of fighting and was shrinking. The third phase was the road back. The Germans were swarming all over the column, and it was taking a beating. Not one vehicle made it back to the American lines. 32 Americans were killed. 35 Americans made it back to the American lines - and only six of those were liberated POW's. The rest were either killed or re-captured. What a failure. It was Patton being Patton.

Some revisionist historians now claim that Patton didn't even know that his son-in-law was at Hammelburg, and that the story was contrived by "Patton-haters." So why is there a group of "Patton-haters" in the first place? There certainly isn't a flock of "Ike-haters."

A couple of Hammelburg sideshows, now:

Guess who was the first prisoner to greet the tanks at the gates of OFLAG-13? It was none other than the man they were all there to save, John K. Waters. It was pure coincidence. Private Waters was wounded and recaptured by the Germans while trying to get back. He survived the war.

Sideshow 2:

At one point in the fighting at the camp, an American priest held Mass. He held it at the POW barracks while the two sides were in the middle of a terrifying tank and infantry fight. An atheist soldier tells this story: he looked up from the ground during the explosions and saw the priest reciting the Latin Mass while bullets and bombs flew all about. The shattered windows and the mix of shadow and sunlight gave the Father the look of a mystical icon as he prayed while the bullets whizzed by his head. The soldier didn't say if this scene converted him to believing in God, but the priest did survive the Mass.

The mission created more new American prisoners than it rescued.

Life magazine had an amazing photo of a jubilant line of Allied POW's emerging from Hammelburg at the very moment of rescue. Few of them could have realized that this was the beginning of a very bad turn of events for most of them. Many who would have been liberated in a month were killed in the running battles. They were like the jailbird who makes his unsuccessful break with two months left on a 20-year stretch. Bad timing, bad decision.

83

Patton's Tour Guide – April 4, 1945

When the U.S. Army liberated its first concentration camp on April 4, 1945, one prisoner was especially helpful. He had the Star of David on his faded blue uniform and he showed the American brass around every nook and cranny of the camp. He pointed out which rooms were for which awful deeds, and pointed out where the bodies were burned and how the entire process worked. He was very helpful.

Ike and Patton stepped back for a private talk:

Ike: There's something bothering me about this guy, George.

Patton: You mean his weight?

Ike: Yes.

That was the end of that military conference. The guy was a little bit on the chubby side. Dwight David Eisenhower personally confronted the man and asked how he got so healthy on a death camp diet? His answer was weak. It didn't take long to expose him for what he was, a Nazi S.S. officer who was trying to escape punishment by playing one of his victims.

Well, since he wanted to be Jewish so bad, Patton decided to let him go be Jewish. Patton ordered the SS slime into the barracks with the real Jews, where he would be able to get a good night's sleep. 900 trillion years of it. The real Jews, of course, murdered the fascist fatso sometime between dusk and dawn.

Just some food for thought.

84
Fort Dix Riot – June 28. 1945

Even though Russia was the ally of the United States, there were nevertheless many Russian prisoners in United States Prisoner of War camps. That's because many Russians, especially Ukrainian-Soviets, had volunteered to serve in the German army. They hated their own Soviet overlords so much that they fought for Hitler. Rommel even spoke of Russian units he deployed in Normandy. When the U.S. Army overran Western Europe they ended up bagging more than a thousand Russian POW's!

In June, 168 Russians at Fort Dix New Jersey (near the center of the state) heard the bad news that they were going to be repatriated (sent back) to the USSR. They knew that this was a death sentence, possibly with brutal beatings along the way. They sent letters to the State Department and other agencies pleading that the United States was virtually executing them by making them go back to the USSR.

Finally, the Russians rioted. It was one of the most bizarre prison riots of all time. The anti-Bolshevik Russians weren't attacking the New Jersey guards, they were attacking themselves! All 168 men tried to kill themselves all at once by seizing weapons with which to do the deed. Three of them managed to die before the guards subdued the rest. The final outcome of this story is that all of the survivors of the suicide riot were indeed forcibly sent back to Russia and were never heard from again.

There had already been a race riot at Fort Dix in 1943. And there's another story about Fort Dix coming up.

85
Empire State Building Disaster – July 28, 1945

It reads like a description of 9/11. A huge state of the art airplane leaves the Boston area at 8:55 a.m. and just after 10:00 a.m. smashes into the 79th floor of the tallest building in New York City. People all over Manhattan hear it and see it and immediately presume that America is under attack. Smoke, fire and death are the order of the day at the tallest building in Manhattan. Parts of the giant airplane go clear through the building and land on the roof of a smaller building on the other side.

This was not 2001, this was July 1945 and the plane was a great big B-25 Mitchell bomber that became lost in a fog and smashed into the Empire State Building, killing 12 people, including the three-man crew on the plane.

86
<u>Drunk With Victory –</u>
<u>September 2, 1945</u>

Japan formally surrendered on board the USS *Missouri* in Tokyo Harbor on September 2, 1945. My father later served on *Mighty Mo* during the Korean War. My grandfather had served on the USS *Maryland* in WWII. To keep the family tradition of naval courage alive, I built a plastic model of the *USS Arizona* during the Vietnam War.

General Douglas MacArthur presided over the 18-minute Japanese surrender proceedings. It was a sunny day, but cool for that time of the year in Tokyo.

Behind him, hanging on the bridge of the great battleship was a huge sign that read "Mission Accomplished." Foreign Minister Shigemitsu signed first for Japan. He seemed to stall before signing, scanning the document in confusion. MacArthur then realized that Shigemitsu had bad eyesight and couldn't find the line to sign on. He whispered to Sutherland to help him, which he did.

One member of the Australian delegation was totally drunk and made disdainful childish goofy faces at the Japanese delegates all afternoon. He was close enough to get under their skin, yet no one ordered him out of the line for being out of line. These Japanese delegates probably remembered the faces that guy made far more than anything else from that day. Decades later they could probably still see those drunken crossed-eyes and the tongue sticking out. Once in a blue moon, alcohol can serve a decent worthwhile purpose.

When the Japanese delegation walked off the ship, a massive flyover of Allied planes rubbed it in. One of the Japanese then noticed, to his chagrin, the collection of Japanese symbols on the side of the Missouri. They were like the decals affixed beneath the window on a fighter plane marking the pilot's kills, except that these were bigger and of greater variety. Mighty Mo had sunk very many Japanese ships, planes, and submarines. This drove home the defeat profoundly.

87
<u>Murder on the Mozart Express - 1946</u>

The situation in Berlin in 1946, with the Allies surrounded by hostile Stalinist territory, was not unique. The situation in Vienna just about matched. The Vienna crisis was resolved in 1955, while the Berlin Crisis went on and on. So the Vienna Crisis, and the short-lived short corridor to Vienna through hostile Red Army territory, has faded from memory. But for nine years after WWII, a lot of people worried that World War III might break out over Austria.

The Allied train that had to "make the run" to and from the American Zone in Germany to Vienna was called the "Mozart Express." Russian troops contrived excuses to stop and board this train, and then mess with it. Anyone gives them a dirty look they beat them up a little. One time, General Mark Clark personally watched Russian soldiers smack one of his aides around the dining car. He soon cabled General Marshall that this would not stand. Marshall e-mailed back that, Clark could get tougher, but be careful, because "the striped pants boys in D.C. don't care about localized incidents."

A few weeks later, a bunch of rough Russians boarded the Mozart Express and tried to intimidate Sergeant Shirley B. Dixon. Shirley pulled a pistol and threatened to use it. They laughed in his face and started pushing him around. Dixon shot one of them dead. Another Russian reached for his rifle and Dixon point his gun around and said the classic, "Anybody else want some of this?" The clacking of the train marked a few tense moments as the political climate changed in Austria.

But only a little.

The military wanted to get tough, the State Department wanted to appease to please, and the two had to find a way to function simultaneously. But at least the military, who wanted to get tough, could at least do so, at least a little bit.

The Russians demanded that the United States hand

Shirley over to them so they could show-try him for murder. Uncle Sam said "Ya nye dumayo" - That's one the few Russians sentences I know, and it means, "I do not think so."

88
The PT Boat That Saved Korea –
June 25, 1950

To me, this is the most amazing and the least known story of the Korean War.

North Korea launched its grand attack on South Korea at 5:00 a.m. on June 25, 1950. But just prior to that, a key incident took place off the southeastern tip of the peninsula. Just before 5:00 a.m. on the 25th of June, a ROK (Republic of South Korea) PT boat spotted two transport ships hovering about off the coast near Pusan. They were obviously not friendly transports. The skipper of the PT boat knew a threat when he saw it. He sped after one transport intending to attack it. That ship went back to North Korea in a hurry. The other ship didn't run. The ROK PT boat fired a torpedo into the stationary transport and sank it.

It turned out that these two transports were each loaded up with 500 North Korean troops. Their mission was to take Pusan by surprise and establish a beachhead there. If these North Korean commandos could hold Pusan, more troops would be sent in quickly.

The North Korean invasion across the 38th parallel was highly successful and the South Korean and UN forces held on famously for dear life in the little box known as the "Pusan perimeter." If those transports had landed that pre-dawn morning, there might not have been a Pusan perimeter for the ROK to fall back on. The North would have been able to squeeze the staggering South on two sides at the southeast corner. Retreating South Korean forces might have been surrounded and demolished somewhere in South Korea.

A single South Korean PT boat may have saved South Korea from being wiped off the map!

This is reminiscent of Pearl Harbor. On December 7, 1941, in the pre-dawn light, a U.S. patrol craft spotted and destroyed a Japanese midget submarine trying to slip into Pearl Harbor. Two hours *later* 363 Japanese planes from six carriers attacked Oahu.

89
Kennedy's Golf Game - 1960

Kennedy knew that he had big golf cleats to fill taking over for the heroic President Eisenhower. How could he forget? Ike had done so much putting in the Oval Office that the floors were severely damaged with cleat marks. Kennedy used to sit in his rocking chair, pondering critical decisions while looking down and seeing Ike's cleat marks; the old man's shadow.

Sometimes visitors would point out the cleat marks and say mean things about Ike, thinking it would endear them to the new president. But that was a turn-off. JFK respected Ike and didn't like cleat shots about his predecessor behind his back. When these coy snipers would leave JFK's presence he would remark that, "They'd shine Ike cleats for him if he were still President."

One day while he was running for President, JFK was golfing in Maryland with his brother RFK and a famous reporter, Joe Alsop. Jack hit a ball that was headed straight for a hole-in-one. Alsop and Robert watched in awe, and yelled "get in!" as the ball was about to go in. But Jack yelled:

"Get out! Get out! Get outa there!"

The ball hit the pole with too much force and rolled away.

Alsop asked him why on earth he was rooting against making a hole-in-one.

Kennedy said:

"I've just spent the last 14 months on the campaign trail criticizing Ike for golfing too much. That's just what I need to read in the press, another golfer in the White House. That could cost me the election!"

Ike's excessive golfing was a major negative for his public image, and that legacy still haunts him. Kennedy knew that the race would be close, and who knows; maybe missing that shot did make a difference. The golf shot that changed history by not going in.

In any case, it is not well known that Kennedy was actually a pretty good golfer, and was better than Ike. John

Kennedy was a good all-round athlete. He was an excellent swimmer, could throw a pretty good long football pass, and place a sharp single to the opposite field in a softball game. But he drew the line at polo. Jackie tried to talk him into learning polo, but he just looked at her in disbelief until she gave up. Football was by far his favorite sport to watch. Kennedy was at least as knowledgeable about the college game as he was of the NFL.

90
The Fan Who Won a
NFL Football Game - 1960

In 2015, with millions of people starving to death every day all over the world, the NFL spent millions of dollars trying to prove that the New England Patriots NFL football team cheated in order to win, by a score of 45-7, in its Championship game over Indianapolis by using footballs in the first half that were under-inflated.

Part of the reason the NFL wanted to punish the Pats is the perception that they have made cheating a part of the team tradition. There was something called "Spygate" a few years ago where the Patriots had guys with binoculars watching other teams' practice, or something like that.

There was a game vs. Miami in the early 70's where the field was a sheet of ice and snow and the Patriots were going to try a field goal to win at the end of the game. Suddenly, on his own initiative, a Walpole State Prison parolee with a snowplow raced across the field during the commercial break and carved out a spot for the placeholder to put the ball down in. The kick was a winner and some people though the Patriots "cheated" that time too.

Then there was the tuck rule game vs the Raiders, where the Pats had cheater's luck.

That "snow plow" guy might have been who you thought I meant by "The Fan That Won an NFL football game," but I've got an even better one than that.

It was November 3, 1961, and the Patriots were playing the Dallas Texans at BU Field. Near the end of a close game the Texans had driven to the goal line dramatically while the unruly fans started to crowd the field. The game had to be stopped repeatedly while the P.A. announcer and the referees urged the fans off the field.

With two seconds left in the game, Dallas was on the Patriots' two-yard line, trailing 28-21. They needed a TD and an extra point to tie the game. Fans were crowded around the end zone. The game had to be stopped and the fans pushed off the field to give Dallas the chance to win, or lose, the game.

Finally the ball was snapped, quarterback Cotton Davidson stepped back; a man was open. Cotton looks, he throws, and it's...batted down...by a fan! And the ref didn't see it! Some punk in a cheap jacket drifted into the secondary from behind the end zone, batted the pass down with his Cotton pickin' hands, and then slipped right back into the stands, all in one smooth-as-silk move. The quarterback yelled at the refs on the way off the field but to no avail.

The Patriots won the game because a fan, literally the 12th man this time, cheated. That guy probably told a thousand people that story and no one believed him.

I heard this story years ago, but I wondered if it was just a legend. But then I saw the footage and the late Billy Sullivan telling the story to Bob Costas on NBC.

91
"No Little Kids!" – December 11, 1960

One of the most popular movies ever made, and deservedly so, is *Scarface,* starring Al Pacino as a small time hitman who rises to drug kingpin status.

A famous and memorable scene (spoiler alert) involved an assassination attempt on a nosy reporter who was writing expose attack stories against the drug lords. A hitman had been sent to NYC from Columbia to do the job and Tony Montana (Pacino) is to serve as the hitman's guide and driver. They have stuck a bomb to the chassis of the target's car, and the hitman riding shotgun will blow it up by radio control. But Tony Montana is very upset because the mark has his wife and kids with him. Scarface wants to call it off,

"I tol you, man, no little kids! I don't need that stuff in my life!"

The hitman tells Tony to shut up and they argue over 15 blocks of Manhattan driving.

"What, it make you feel like big man? Killing a woman and little kids? No way!"

"Shut up!" says Alberto in Spanish.

Finally Tony calls off the hit by pulling a pistol and shooting the hitman in the head.

"I tried to tell you! No little kids! But you wouldn't listen. Look at you now!"

A similar scene happened to John Kennedy when he was President-elect in December of 1960 at Palm Beach (without the gory ending).

A 73-year old stalker from Belmont, New Hampshire hated Kennedy because he felt that father Joe Kennedy had bought the election. Richard Pavlick worked against Kennedy in New Hampshire to no avail and he decided that if he couldn't prevent Kennedy's election, he would prevent his inauguration.

Pavlick stuck seven sticks of dynamite on the bumper of his own car. It was set up to go off with a contact trigger.

Pavlick waited patiently outside of the Kennedy home in Palm Beach, Florida in the early morning hours. At 8:33 a.m. John F. Kennedy walked outside his home and toward his car to drive to Mass at Saint Edgar's Church. Richard Pavlick started the engine. It was going to be an assassination suicide.

Tense movie music please.

Just as Pavlick was about to put the engine into drive and ram Kennedy's car, Jacqueline walked out to the car, carrying the loudly-crying newborn John-John. Pavlick knew he had to call it off, just like *Scarface*.

If Jack had been alone he would have died. If Pavlick had the conscience of Alberto, JFK would have died.

The scene is so close to the *Scarface* scene in NYC that I have to wonder if Oliver Stone based it on Pavlick. I certainly wouldn't put it past 'The Stoner.' And we all know that Oliver Stone has an avid interest in JFK.

Pavlik was released from a nut house in 1966.

92

Ham in Space – January 31, 1961

Kennedy's tenure wasn't two weeks old when the United States sent a rocket into outer space with a living creature on board. It was the USA that sent the first mammal into outer space, not the Russians. On January 31, a Sammy Redstone rocket sent a chimpanzee by the name of Ham into a low earth orbit for 16 minutes.

Actually, the charming chimp didn't get a name until he returned safely. NASA figured that if the chimp got a cute name and became a national celebrity, then died in a mission failure; that would be bad. So an unnamed chump chimp went up and returned a champ chimp named Ham. The creature came back alive after mission accomplished. He Hammed it up as a guest on the Jack Paar show in March.

93

Sukharno Visits Washington - 1961

Most Americans today have never heard of this historical man, but President Sukharno (one-name) of Indonesia was very famous during the Kennedy era. The average housewife in Muncie knew who Sukharno was.

One of the most volatile and difficult countries that Kennedy had to deal with in foreign affairs was Indonesia. It is a huge country made up of 17,508 islands in South Asia. More than 10,000 of these islands have no human beings. What a place to go read.

Indonesia was a crossroad in geography and ideology. It wasn't Communist, but it had a big Communist movement. It had the largest Muslim population in the world (and still does), but was not exporting radical Islam. Indonesia also had enormous Christian and Hindu populations. It claimed to embrace democracy, but it was ruled by a dictator. There was a lot of political trouble in Indonesia in the Kennedy "Thousand Days."

Indonesia was coveted by the east, the west, and to a lesser extent, by the Indonesians. This country didn't want to be a pawn in the Cold War. It was too strong and powerful to play that role willingly, but the role was hard to avoid, since it was a fact, not a choice.

But Indonesia was also definitely "neutral," which in Kennedy's time was not a good thing. Neutral to Washington meant tilted against the United States, in spite of your claims to the contrary. Kennedy's globe was like the W. Bush globe. You were either for U.S. or against U.S., in spite of pleas by some Kennedy cabinet liberals to change that thinking.

President Sukharno made a state visit to Washington in early 1961 and shocked the Kennedy team with his bizarre and arrogant attitude. He arrived at the airport and immediately asked to have prostitutes sent to his hotel.

Folks, I am not making this up.

When Rusk and Hillsman wanted to discuss South Asian politics, Sukharno changed the subject to the sizzling figures of movie stars Marylyn Monroe and Gina

Lollibridgida. It never stopped. "All the guy wanted to talk about," complained Hillsman later, "was dames."

Then Sukharno had the audacity to suggest to Dean Rusk that Jacqueline Kennedy pay a state visit to Indonesia, and that it must be without President Kennedy.

I'm completely serious.

Rusk sent a crisp note to Kennedy saying that he was not about to authorize such a trip. Kennedy did not respond to the Rusk memo, which indicated he agreed with its delicate content.

The Kennedy team was elated to drive Sukharno to the airport and put him on a plane back to Indonesia.

Kennedy told Powers that he was shocked at Sukharno's bad behavior. "I'm not as pure as the Vermont snow," Kennedy said, "But how can a man let the ladies interfere with his ability to conduct international relations? It's beyond me."

Hillsman chimed in, "Man cannot live by broad alone."

Just for the record the United States government denied Sukharno's request for prostitutes.

Former President Bill Clinton is currently writing a biography of Sukharno titled "*Sukharno the Great.*"

94
JFK is Mad at Robert Frost - 1962

The official poet laureate of the Kennedy Administration was Robert Frost. He is still one of the few household names among the poets, ranking up there with McKuen, Hank Longfellow, Shelly, Chillingsworth, Angelou, and Serpico (see Pablo's latest poem protesting the U.S. bombing titled 'Barak O-Bomber').

In the first week of September 1962, Rob Frost accepted an invitation from Nikita Krushchev to visit the Soviet Union. Krushchev claimed to be a fan of Frost's poetry. Mo Udall was going to Moscow for talks, and maybe Frost could tag along for more friendly talks, suggested Krushchev. Frost asked Bobby Kennedy to ask Jack if it would be okay. The word came back that a meeting in Russia between Frost and Krushchev could do no harm and might offer some valuable insight into Russian thinking, especially regarding the growing crisis over Cuba. Perhaps Nicky would let his guard down while talking to the famous artist. JFK gave the OK. The Frost trip to Russia was front page news for 10 days in America.

But Frost got fairly ill when he arrived in Russia, which was not surprising since he was in his 80's and only had a year left to live; one mile to go before he sleeps.

Krushchev actually visited Robert's Russian sickbed and had three long chats with the great poet. Nicky knew that Frost was an ear to Kennedy, so he told the Yankee that the USSR felt very threatened by the presence of American missiles all around them. Frost listened with all the political insight of a poet. The poet was shaking a little. Frost had the chills.

Frost landed at Idlewild Airport in NYC on September 9, 1962. Frost and Udall gave an airport press conference about the trip to Russia. Frost said:

"Krushchev told me that you liberals in America will never fight. You'll stand around for years deciding what to do and in the end you'll do nothing."

Kennedy was watching this on TV at the White House and he became angry. He got up from his rocking chair and complained furiously to Sorenson:

"Why did Frost have to say that? What the hell is wrong with him? That's exactly what my critics are saying about me over here. I send him over there to help us and he comes back and says this? Is he addled or something?"

The big stars of the press, film and the arts were frequent guests at Camelot. Sinatra stops by to say hello; that sort of thing. But Robert Frost lost his key to the kingdom with his idle wild talk in September of 62. The next several times he tried to see Kennedy in person he got a Frosty reception. One time, Kennedy's Personal Secretary Evelyn Lincoln told Frost that Kennedy was on a trip to the Congo, even though Frost saw Kennedy in his rocking chair in the second story window talking to someone.

When Frost turned to ice in January of 1963, Kennedy did not attend the funeral and said a short perfunctory few words to the press expressing formal praise.

95
<u>Convert - 1966</u>

A POW story from Nam.

An American prisoner at the Hanoi Hilton was a devout atheist. After a day of torture he came back to a fellow prisoner who asked him:

"How did it go?"

"How did it go? I've found religion. I've been converted."

"Well, what religion have you been converted to?"

"All of them."

96
An Attack on Liberty – June 1967

On June 8, 1967, during the Arab-Israeli War, the USS *Liberty* was cruising in international waters in the Mediterranean Sea when Israeli fighter jets attacked without provocation. It was the *Panay* (1937) all over again, but this time a supposedly friendly power was attacking an American ship without warning. The *Liberty* was clearly marked with United States flags. The attack continued for some time. It wasn't enough to attack the U.S. ship with Israel's Mirage fighters. The Israelis then sent in several torpedo boats to continue the attack!

Liberty was badly damaged, but did not sink. The Israeli Defense Force had murdered thirty-four American sailors. Seventy-five were wounded, including Commander McGonagle who continued to relay details of the attack back to base while down on the floor and bleeding on the bridge.

The Israeli government apologized for the attack, but never adequately explained why it happened. Was this revenge for U.S. refusal to take Israel's side in this war, or maybe payback for U.S. betrayal in the Suez Crisis of 1956?

The Israelis claimed that they mistook the ship for an Egyptian horse-freighter that had a similar silhouette. Right.

If they did do it deliberately, the next obvious question is why? Why attack the one nation on earth that had always supported Israel both politically and materially?

The answer may be very diabolical. Several observers swear that <u>unmarked</u> Mirage planes delivered the attack.

The conclusion is inescapable. The Israelis wanted to make it look like an attack on a U.S. ship by Egyptian planes. In this way they hoped to draw the United States into the war on the side of Israel. They hoped to sink *Liberty* and leave no survivors to tell the story. *Liberty* foiled their plan by staying afloat and hobbling back to port.

Dean Rusk, the Secretary of State, never accepted the

Israeli explanation of mistaken identity. There are a few hundred other expert opinions that also doubt Israel's veracity. Only Robert McNamara seems to have believed their explanation, which is perfect since McNamara has made a lifelong career out of being wrong on everything (on the eve of the 1991 Gulf War he warned Congress that, "we were going to suffer thousands and thousands and thousands of casualties!").

There is no statute of limitations on the crime of murder. Several Israeli participants have allegedly admitted that it was not an accident.

The Israeli government to this day, of course, insists that the attack was an accident. *Liberty* was allegedly in the vicinity where an Egyptian warship had recently been shelling Israeli troop positions in the Sinai. The attack was explained as in response to that sea to shore barrage, and the *Liberty* was mistaken for an enemy.

The case is mysterious. It is easy to imagine a callous political decision being made to do this by Israel's top officials, but it is hard to imagine that so many individual members of the Israeli Defense Forces would knowingly attack a loyal ally as part of a fantastic disinformation operation.

All this doesn't change my feeling about the 1967 War. Little David Israel picked up all the Arab Goliaths at the same time and threw them out of the ring. Tremendous.

97

The True Story of Chappaquiddick - 1969

The story of the death of Mary Jo Kopechne in the back of Senator Edward Kennedy's Oldsmobile in July of 1969 was an event that changed history. If not for the incident at Chappaquiddick, a small island to the east of Martha's Vineyard, Ted Kennedy would have been the Democratic Nominee for President in 1972. He probably would have beaten Richard Nixon and probably would have been president twice, from 1973 to 1981.

First the basic version that Senator Edward Kennedy told the world in his televised address while in a neck brace.

Ted Kennedy was on vacation on Martha's Vineyard in July of 1969 and his little group was staying at a little cottage on little Chappaquiddick Island, a one minute ferry ride due east from "The Vineyard."

The happily married Senator was in a car with a young single attractive woman of 22 named Mary Jo Kopechne. They were just driving around Chappaquiddick late at night making small talk. They drove down to the end of Dyke Road, which leads to the small Dyke Bridge. Somehow his huge black Oldsmobile hit the bridge at a bad angle and went into Poucha Pond. The Olds turned upside down. Ted got out of the car and swam to the surface. Then he dove under to try and find and save Mary Jo. He dove down again and again until exhausted. He couldn't fight off the swift currents and couldn't pull her out of the car. Finally, tired beyond his capacity, he ran the length of Dyke Road and made it back to the cottage where he told his companions what happened, and they did not call the police. His memory of the evening was clouded from the stress, and he was "not under the influence of liquor."

I had a stand-up gig on Martha's Vineyard in the mid-1990's and I grabbed a paperback copy of "*The Bridge at Chappaquiddick*," by Jack Olsen. I took the ferry to "Chappy" and rode a rented moped bike and made my way to the infamous Bridge. I had read most of the book, and I finished that last chapter while sitting within sight of the bridge.

The thing that strikes you when looking at the bridge is how small and steeply curved it is. There are no guard rails, and it's as rounded as half a basketball. No one in their right mind would want to drive over it at all, for any reason. There's only sandy beach on the other side. It looks like it's strictly for official business by someone driving a government jeep. No one in a big Oldsmobile would ever want to drive over that bridge.

This makes the Jack Olsen theory of what really happened make perfect sense, and makes it - Olsen's theory - the only logical explanation for what happened.

The only way to solve the puzzle was by process of deduction. Evidence was scant at best. The thing that most discredits Kennedy's story was that early the following morning he was seen at the Chappaquiddick Ferry landing chatting it up cheerfully in dry clothes. He didn't look distraught, or disheveled. Then someone walked up to him and told him that they just fished his car out of Poucha Pond and there was a dead girl in it. Kennedy turned white and by the end of the day the world got the explanation through the press conference he later gave on live TV. No drinking, he tried to save her, his memory is fuzzy.

Jack Olsen was there for all the 1969 hearings at the Edgartown Police Station and Court House and he put the pieces together.

While Ted was driving around Chappaquiddick with Mary Jo late at night, a police cruiser followed him. This is confirmed by the cop who followed him. Kennedy took a right turn onto Dyke Road, an incredibly horrible dirt road with deeper ruts than any road I can ever remember dealing with ever. He could have turned left onto a paved road. The cop thought it was odd, but didn't follow him down the Dyke Road. Kennedy hadn't done anything wrong (the cop knew whose car it was) and the cop also didn't want to ruin his cruiser going down Dyke Road. If Kennedy wanted to ruin his Oldsmobile by driving down that awful dirt road, whatever.

But for all Ted Kennedy knew, the cop was going to

change his mind and head down Dyke Road to bother him. He drove down Dyke Road a couple of hundred feet and told Mary Jo something to this effect:

"Look, I can't be caught with you like this. It will be the end of my career. You drive the car and I'll hop out and hide in the woods. Drive down to the end of the road and if he arrests you for drunk driving we can take care of it later. After an hour or so, if the coast is clear, I'll walk down and find you near the bridge. But I cannot get caught in this car with you."

Mary Jo agreed and Kennedy hid in the woods. Mary Jo was 5-feet, 2-inches and Ted Kennedy was 6-feet, 2-inches. She was intoxicated. When she came to the Dyke Bridge she went to hit the brake, she had trouble reaching it and, in a panic move, instead hit the accelerator real hard. That car hit the Bridge at 45-miles per hour. No one probably ever did that in the history of the Bridge. The Olds hit the bridge with such force that it not only went into the Pond upside down, it reversed direction! No one in their right mind would try to go over that bridge at even 10 miles per hour.

So Kennedy waits, and waits, and then makes the 1.5 mile walk to the end of Dyke Road. When he gets there he sees nothing. Everything looks normal. It's a quiet summer night at Poucha Pond.

The tide had risen in the Pond so that Kennedy could not see the submerged car. He looked around, scratched his head, gave up, and walked back up Dyke Road to their rented cottage where he told his friends he couldn't find Mary Jo. They all presumed she had gone for a drunken joy ride up the beach and would turn up after her hangover wore off.

Next morning Teddy's ready to take the ferry back to Martha's Vineyard when he finds out that his car has just been pulled out of Poucha Pond "with a dead girl in it."

His cover story was so weak that few people really believed him. But no one had a solid alternative explanation either. Fortunately for Kennedy, few Americans have ever been to Chappaquiddick Island and the Dyke Bridge, because if they had, they would have, like me, thought to themselves, "it makes no sense that they were trying to cross that bridge in the first place."

When I got back to the mainland I wrote to author Jack Olsen, and to my surprise he wrote me back and then we had some telephone conversations. He was miffed with MSNBC because they had just done their own TV investigation of the event and had come to the same conclusion that Kennedy had never been in the car. MSNBC agreed with Olsen's theories to the last detail. But they never mentioned Jack Olsen or his book or the fact that they weren't the first ones to come to this startling conclusion.

Jack Olsen helped me get an article published in Sports Illustrated, but that's another story for another book.

No one can prove that this is the true story of what happened that night in 1969, but Ted Kennedy's version of it makes little sense at all. For example, people often asked why he didn't knock on anyone's door to have them telephone for help when he made his way back to his rented cottage. Several homes had lights on and he just walked on past in his soaking clothes another two miles while she held her breath in his car. He had no explanation in his TV address why he had behaved so illogically and irresponsibly. The brilliant Senator who knew the last detail of every Bill being presented before Congress felt disoriented that night and was not thinking clearly. He offered no explanation as to why he didn't knock on anyone's door on the way back.

As for his claim that he had not been drinking at the time, that's crying funny.

Many people thought from then on that Ted Kennedy was "a manslaughterer" who had left Mary Jo Kopechne to die. He should have been prosecuted for a number of serious criminal charges, but with his political connections, he got away with it. The hatred for Ted ran deep. The vicious jokes began and have never stopped to this day. You can still make a joke on stage about the late Senator's drinking and get a laugh. Or at least I can.

The incident at Poucha Pond ruined his chance for the Presidency.

In a way, it makes him less of a bad guy if Olsen's version is the truth. But Kennedy would rather have some people think he got away with manslaughter, than have everyone know he was a drunken cheater; because the latter, unlike the former, would be an undeniable certainty, and would have meant the end of his career. This was before the Bill Clinton era where one could be an overt cheater and not lose his or her political base.

We can only use our imaginations to wonder how it all would have worked out if TK had just told the God's honest truth. But then again, he was a politician, and they don't specialize in that.

98

Greenwich Village Bomb Intended for Fort Dix – March 6, 1970

Tonight's forecast, bombs. The Weathermen left-wing radicals were up to their old tricks on March 6, 1970, building bombs to kill squares with.

They killed three of themselves when a bomb they were building to harm others went off by accident. Hoo-ray! It happened at 18 West 11th Street in the Village. The bomb set the building on fire and tore it up real bad.

The Greenwich Village bomb was a big one. It took down a building. Those whacky Weathermen were building themselves quite a big bomb.

And what were they planning on doing with that bomb?

The answer to that is important. Up until then, the American Weathermen lefty extremists had bombed only empty buildings of "the Establishment," like banks, government agencies, insurance companies, stand-up comedy clubs, or an empty military recruiting station. But the March madness that went off by accident on March 6, 1970 had bigger intentions.

This time the Weathermen were going to kill people. We're not talking of bombing an office with a few people in it; killing two or three fascist pigs. These lefties were planning on setting off the biggest bomb they had ever built at a place with the greatest potential for maximum death and bloodshed. They were going to blow up a crowded dance hall at Fort Dix, NJ. NCO dance night was the target date. The Weathermen were going to do a mini-World Trade Center on their own country, supposedly in order to protest the Vietnam War.

If that bomb had gone off like it was supposed to, it might have killed more than 100 decent Americans.

And just imagine if it had gone off as planned. Imagine how all of American history would have been changed by that! In May, the left gained a momentum that never died with Kent State. But if the Greenwich Bomb went off at Fort Dix in March, there would have been no Kent State incident. That bomb would have set the left and the anti-war movement back. The massacre of 100 people at Fort Dix would have created a sea change in the American political dynamic. The political center would have gone from left-leaning to right-leaning in one day. It would have disgraced extreme leftism in general, big time. Close to half the victims would have been women. Imagine the national martyrs these poor people would have become? There might have been a few children there too.

Instead the bomb went off by accident on the perps (again, hoo-ray!), and then Kent State swung the center much further over to the hard left instead. What a decisive moment in history; that bomb going off by accident. These loony-lefties blew themselves up, but saved the left by doing so! If they had bombed Fort Dix, they might have prolonged the Vietnam War!

Bill Ayers and other ex-Weathermen now claim that the three who died at the Townhouse were an extremist splinter group, and that he did not agree at the time with their new plans to actually kill people. I say if you're part of a group that keeps advocating violence, a group you helped found, one that already bombed 14 various buildings where a janitor or wino sleeping inside could easily have died, and if you backed the Black Panthers in their proclamations to kill all police officers at random, then it's hard to distance yourself from the Fort Dix massacre that almost happened.

The Weathermen became the "Weather Underground" after the Greenwich Townhouse Bomb went up. The FBI discovered the original intent of the bomb and put the rest of the Weathermen and women under a cloud of indictments. Now they were wanted for conspiracy to commit murder. They had to hide, go underground. They went underground for years while the FBI hunted them down. Some of them cut their hair and wore glasses they didn't need. Most of them eventually turned themselves in after the passage of enough years gave them hope for some leniency. The Establishment put them on trial and gave them a couple of years on average; not bad for conspiracy to commit mass murder with all the other bombings added in.

I have no recollection of this news event. It is seldom

mentioned in general histories so it's almost a new and startling event to learn about. Few Americans know of the Greenwich Townhouse Explosion, and only some of those few know that the bomb under construction was supposed to kill people. One major history website has this to say about the bombers:

"No one was killed in these bombings, because the bombers always called in an advanced warning. However, three members of the Weather Underground died on March 6, 1970, when the house in which they were constructing the bombs exploded."

That's misleading. The second sentence is disconnected from the first, but this makes it seem that they connect. This is convoluted apologism, although probably not deliberate. Like I say, few people really know what they were really trying to do with that March 6, 1970 bomb. That quote was taken from the History Channel Website. My source on this is Weatherman Mark Rudd.

Dustin Hoffman lived on 20 W. 11th, right next door to the blown up building. He is visible in the background in some of the photos of the street scene aftermath. He asked a fireman what caused the explosion and the man responded, "plastics."

99
<u>The Photographer Speaks - 1975</u>

On May 12, 1975, Cambodian naval patrol forces seized a U.S. freighter, the *Mayaguez,* and held its American crew hostage. They took ship and crew to a small Cambodian island off the mainland. The *Mayaguez* became an international crisis that dominated the headlines for many days. This was extra bitter for America as it had just watched Cambodia and South Vietnam fall to the Communists. Now the Communists were adding insult to injury by attacking American merchant ships.

As the *Mayaguez* days went on, the Ford security team met often. One National Security Team meeting examined several levels of military response options as U.S. ships zeroed in on the *Mayaguez*. At the very least, the U.S. Navy would employ whatever means necessary to rescue the crew and then scoot home. Another option was to rescue the crew and then give Cambodia a multi-megaton taste of U.S. B-52 bombers as punishment, and as a warning to all nations that the tiger still had teeth.

Kissinger, Ford, and Defense Secretary James Schlesinger were arguing over these options. Schlesinger was against military force over and above what was necessary to complete the rescue mission. Jim never backed down from his opinion that adding punitive raids to the rescue mission was just senseless killing that wasn't going to make a bit of difference in the political situation in Southeast Asia or in America's relationship to the region, except perhaps to make it worse. The rest of the guys told Schlesinger he was wrong. They said that this was a perfect moment to show the world that the United States would not to be pushed around anywhere on earth. Just because the United States had withdrawn from Southeast Asia did not mean that it had become the laughable target for any aggression anyone felt like trying. Kissinger and others said that the seizure of the *Mayaguez* was a provocation and should be answered in kind, and just getting the hostages back didn't fit the bill. The argument reached a deadlock and exhausted itself. "Slesh" had courage and what he said made sense. But what the others said made sense too. No one could win or lose the argument. Ford looked at everyone and no one had an answer.

Then, to everyone's shock, an unauthorized voice spoke up. He was a man named Kennerly whose job title was photographer. He had often been present taking pictures at important national security meetings. Kennerly was a man in his 20's and had never spoken at one of these meetings before and had no formal right to do so. The mere fact that he was speaking had everyone listening in shocked silence:

"Has anyone ever considered that this might be the act of a local Cambodian commander who has just taken it into his own hands to halt any ship that comes by? Has anyone stopped to think that he might not have gotten his orders from Phnom Penh? If that's what happened, you know, you can blow the whole place away and it's not gonna make any difference. Everyone here has been talking about Cambodia as if it were a traditional government, like France. We have trouble with France, we just pick up the telephone and call. We know who to talk to. But I was in Cambodia just two weeks ago, and it's not that kind of government at all. We don't even know who the leadership is. Has anyone ever considered that?"

The argument resumed, based on this new point. After 20 more minutes, Ford announced that what Kennerly said made sense and the meeting adjourned! The photographer's cogent comment helped persuade Ford not to launch massive retaliatory air raids on the Cambodian mainland.

100
<u>The Storm That Made a President</u>

After attending Eureka College in 1932, Ronald Reagan went to Chicago to literally knock on the door of every local radio station to try to break into broadcasting. But Chicago gave him a cold wind and it was back to Dixon to regroup. It was a greatly depressing time for most Americans.

RR then followed some sound advice and tried again to break into radio at the ground floor, this time in the small tri-city area to his southwest. At WOC in Davenport, Iowa, he finally caught a break and soon was live-broadcasting Big Ten college football games for Iowa U. But after three games the gig was up and it was back to Dixon.

A job opened up for Ron Reagan at WHO in Des Moines, a step up from Davenport. Ronald was an all-purpose disc jockey and announcer and, in addition, was employed to "broadcast" Chicago Cub major league baseball games. What he did was create the illusion that he was broadcasting live, but it was really just re-creating the plays that were sent in over the telegraph. I cannot understand how people were so stupid as to fall for this. He was honestly trying to trick them and it actually worked. What a bunch of rubes!

As lame as this part of his WHO duties may seem today (and shame on those who write that Reagan "was a major league play by play broadcaster") it helped get Reagan off the farm and off to Hollywood. Here's how it happened.

Ronald pitched to WHO the ingenious idea that they should pay him to accompany the Chicago Cubs to spring training camp in Southern California. By really getting to know the team he could do a better job at phony broadcasting when the season started.

To his surprise and delight they accepted the idea and in 1937 Reagan was assigned to Cubby-camp on Catalina Island.

Now comes an example of weather changing history.

One day, Reagan was in LA waiting to take the next boat to Catalina when a bad storm hit. All boats back to

Catalina, 26 miles across the sea, were grounded. A friend who worked at a big Hollywood studio called Reagan and said, "You got nothing to do today. Why not come on over with me to the studio? Maybe I'll even get you a screen test, you'd be a natural."

So Reagan used his storm-day to visit a friend at a movie studio. The screen test was a success. In no time flat Reagan was acting full-time for serious money. He was in with the in-crowd. He was soon under contract and appearing in movies. At the height of the Depression, Ronald Reagan was rich. He called his parents to come west. He could take care of them now. And he forgot all about how the Cubs were doing.

And he was great in *The Hasty Heart*.

101
<u>The Nurse - 1981</u>

When in 1981 John Hinckley shot President Ronald Reagan in Washington, the injured President walked into the ER of the George Washington University Hospital, waved hello to everyone like it was just a scratch and then collapsed to the ground semi-conscious.

Secret Serviceman Jerry Parr had shoved Reagan into the limo amidst the chaos of the shooting and thought the President had simply suffered a couple of broken ribs. Parr wanted at first to go to the White House where a medical staff could treat him, but when Reagan coughed up some blood, Parr insisted they go to the nearest hospital.

When the doctors finally realized he had been shot, they discovered that the bullet was in a dangerous place and removing it was going to be a threat to the President's life. The procedure was a success, but it was a close call.

Throughout most of the crucial two hours, Reagan was semi-conscious and, while unable to talk, was aware of what was going on around him.

A nurse took some daring initiative and held his hand through most of this. No one noticed her. Reagan speaks in his memoir of this gesture with something beyond mere appreciation. He felt almost as if it saved his life. That little human connection, her compassion with this gesture kept his faith alive that somehow everything was going to be okay.

President Reagan never found out who this nurse was. He wanted to thank her, and in his memoirs he did. The fact that she chose to remain anonymous is a beautiful thing. She could have made herself famous. It took a lot of courage for her to decide that he wasn't a powerful president that no one dared to touch, but just a powerless wounded human being who was entitled to just as much compassion as any other patient. It took a lot of inner beauty to choose to remain anonymous. What a credit to her profession!

Afterward

Sources are listed on my website
comedianmikedonovan.com.

This Book is Dedicated to
All the Horses Who Died in War

37350492R00138

Made in the USA
Middletown, DE
26 November 2016